MORE MEMORIES OF
LEEDS

TRUE NORTH BOOKS
DEAN CLOUGH
HALIFAX
WEST YORKSHIRE
HX3 5AX
TEL 01422 344344

THE PUBLISHERS WOULD LIKE TO THANK THE
FOLLOWING COMPANIES FOR SUPPORTING THE
PRODUCTION OF THIS BOOK

MAIN SPONSOR
LEEDS HOSPITAL FUND LIMITED

ALLIED DOMECQ INNS

T.F. & J.H. BRAIME (HOLDINGS) PLC

JOHN CATLOW LIMITED

CENTRAL MOTOR AUCTIONS PLC

THE CORN EXCHANGE SHOPPING CENTRE

THOMAS DANBY COLLEGE

EVANS PLC

FIRTH RAY & PROSSER LIMITED

JAMES HARE LIMITED

LEEDS CANAL BASIN (DEV) LIMITED

LEEDS CIVIC THEATRE

ABRAHAM MOON & SONS LIMITED

OILGEAR TOWLER LIMITED

PELICAN ENGINEERING CO. LIMITED

PENNINE CASTINGS LIMITED

S. ROSS & CO. LIMITED

ROTHERA & BRERETON LIMITED

JOHN STANSFIELD LIMITED

STOREY EVANS AND CO. LIMITED

W.H. & H.M. YOUNG LIMITED

First published in Great Britain by True North Books
Dean Clough
Halifax HX3 5AX
1998

ISBN 1 900 463 12 1

Introduction

Welcome to *Memories of Leeds*, a look back on some of the places, events and people in the city which have shaped our lives over a period of around half a century. The following pages are brought to life by the selection of images from the not-too-distant past, chosen according to their ability to rekindle fond memories of days gone by and show how people used to shop, work and play in the place where they grew up.

The bustling Kirkgate area of Leeds pictured during the mid 1950s.

The chosen period covered is one which generally contains events within the memory of a large number of people in Leeds - this is not a book about crinolines or bowler-hats! Neither is *Memories of Leeds* a work of local history in the normal sense of the term. It has far more to do with entertainment than serious study, but we hope you will agree it is none the worse for that. It is hoped that the following pages will prompt readers own memories of Leeds from days gone by - and we are always delighted to hear from people who can add to the information contained in the captions so that we can enhance future reprints of the book. Many local companies and organisations have allowed us to study their archives and include their history - and fascinating reading it makes too.

The present-day guardians of the companies concerned are proud of their products, the achievements of their people and the hard work of their forefathers whose efforts created these long established firms in the first place. We are pleased to play our part by making it possible for them to share their history with a wider audience.

When we began compiling *Memories of Leeds* several months ago we anticipated that the task would be a pleasurable one, but our expectations were greatly surpassed. There is a growing appetite for all things 'nostalgic' and we are pleased to have played a small part in swelling the number of images and associated information available to the growing number of enthusiasts.

There is much talk in modern times about the regeneration of the local economy, the influx of new industries and the challenge of attracting new enterprise from other regions to Leeds. And quite right too. We could, however, make the mistake of thinking that the changes are all happening *now,* but the reality is that there have always been major developments going on in the town. 'Change' is relentless and the photographs on the pages in the book serve to remind us of a mere a selection of them.

Some of the images fall outside the qualification we describe as 'within living memory', but most of these will be familiar to us, either because they concern an event described to us by a close relative, or they feature monuments such as major roads or buildings we simply felt compelled to mention. Whatever the view taken on the boundaries which separate 'history', 'nostalgia' and the present time we should all invest a little time occasionally to reflect on the past and the people and events which made our city what it is today. *Memories of Leeds* has been a pleasure to compile, we sincerely hope you enjoy reading it.

Happy memories!

PHOTOGRAPH COMPILATION/COVER DESIGN.................MARK SMITH

CAPTIONS RESEARCH AND COMPILATION.................PHIL HOLLAND

DESIGNERS......................MANDY WALKER AND NICKY BRIGHTON

COPYWRITERS.......................PAULINE BELL AND PEGGY BURNS

BUSINESS DEVELOPMENT EDITOR......................GARETH MARTIN

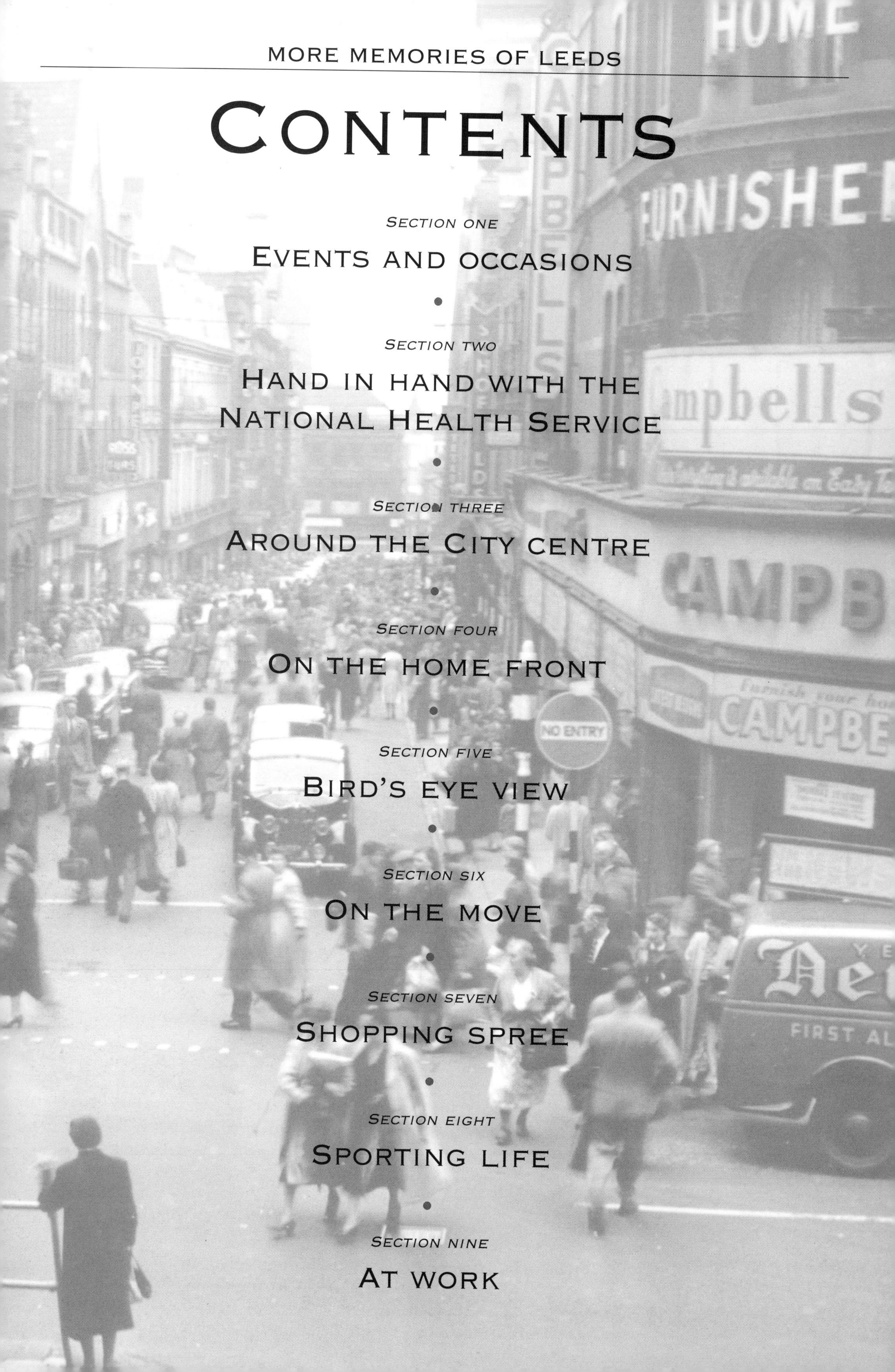

CONTENTS

SECTION ONE

EVENTS AND OCCASIONS

•

SECTION TWO

HAND IN HAND WITH THE NATIONAL HEALTH SERVICE

•

SECTION THREE

AROUND THE CITY CENTRE

•

SECTION FOUR

ON THE HOME FRONT

•

SECTION FIVE

BIRD'S EYE VIEW

•

SECTION SIX

ON THE MOVE

•

SECTION SEVEN

SHOPPING SPREE

•

SECTION EIGHT

SPORTING LIFE

•

SECTION NINE

AT WORK

Events and occasions

Victory in Europe celebrations were not confined to street parties and public houses. Every workplace was decorated with flags and bunting to mark the end of the war in Europe in May 1945. The six year conflict had transformed the lives of people throughout Britain. People in Leeds were no exception, with around 110,000 members of the population directly involved in military action and virtually every other adult fully engaged in indus-trial activities on the Home Front. This picture is interesting not least of which for the very wide range of ages of the women workers in the room. The war had virtually eradicated unemployment and provided meaningful, responsible work for many who could previously only dream of it. The end of the war was extremely welcome, but for many people it meant the end of their employment as the menfolk returned home.

Above: The most effective wartime leader of all time, and Britain's best-known Prime Minister, Winston Churchill is shown leaving Leeds Civic Hall after a popular visit in the 1940s. The respected political figure is seen with the love of his life Clementine. Churchill's political career was remarkable. He had first stood for Parliament in 1899 in Oldham. He lost, but returned victorious in the following year. Churchill's rise to wartime leadership over the next four decades is well documented. It seems surprising, looking back, that the first election after the war saw him rejected by the electorate as the Labour Party swept into power. Never a quitter, Churchill kept going, and won the 1951 General Election ......at the age of 77

Top: Some rather uncertain 'V' signs give a clue to the reason that this street party was being held in the Manor Grove area of the city. This Victory in Japan celebration took place in September 1945 after the Japanese forces had surrendered.

It is obvious from this picture that there were not enough tables and chairs for the adults to enjoy the food that had been put out, but an exception had been made for four or five young men - one of whom was in a wheelchair. Perhaps these men were recently-returned war heroes?

In the background, to the right, are the streets' brick built air raid shelters. Leeds endured several serious bombing raids which caused loss of life, but thankfully nothing like the carnage that affected London or many other large British cities.

Above: When victory came after six long years of the Second World War it was the signal for celebrations the like of which had never been seen before. Flags and bunting was strewn from every possible vantage point and the 'V' sign which had been made famous by Prime Minister Winston Churchill was painted on anything and everything. This charming scene from around 50 years ago depicts people, mainly women and children, on an inner-city street in Leeds. They pose for the camera, little knowing that the snap would be published when even the smallest children featured her were considering their retirement plans! No doubt the group would later enjoy one of the hundreds of street parties in the district. Perhaps the adults would attend one of the many dances in town in the evening. Of course, the celebrations were tinged with sadness and overshadowed by thoughts of the loved ones who would never see their *Leeds* again.

A solitary police officer keeps the crowds in order at the annual Quarry Hill Carnival. This picture was taken to record the winners in the childrens' fancy dress competition - and don't they all look tremendous! It was always a difficult job for the judges trying to pick the winners from up to 500 children who entered the popular competition each year. This picture was taken in 1948 and the theme of the winning entry was "That's what little girls are made of."

Right: A charming picture dating from 1952 and showing the Carnival Queen being crowned at Quarry Hill Flats. This was always a popular element of the carnival's activities. The Quarry Hill Tenants Association took pride in the social and other activities they undertook. The organisation was founded in 1946 and continued until 1962. In 1949, the height of its success (if measured in terms of membership) there were almost 500 members of the Association. The Carnival began in 1947 and was run annually until 1962. At around £100 per annum it was the biggest expense of the year according to the accounts produced by the Association, and it was always one of the most popular. The Carnival included a tea party at St. James' Hall for the children of the members followed by a concert party given by the children at the flats.

Below: The crowning of the Quarry Hill Carnival Queen was always eagerly awaited. Fourteen-year-old Alma Brown of Oastler House was the Queen in 1951 and she is featured here with attendants Mollie Evers and Pat Wilkinson. Alma attended Roseville Secondary Modern School and found herself with the honour after the originally-chosen Carnival Queen resigned unexpectedly. This was brought about when Sonia Craffe's parents decided to move house to Seacroft.

*Her Majesty the Queen's
visit to Leeds in 1958 was the
cause of tremendous excitement
and celebration throughout the
City. We have to remember that this
was only around five years after the
Coronation, and that feelings towards the
popular young monarch and her young family
were at their peak. Thousands of local people
turned out to greet the royal visitor and express
their loyalty and affection. This picture shows four
gleaming black limousines gliding up The Headrow,
followed by six highly-polished police cars detailed to
provide security and traffic management if necessary. Several
thousand people lined The Headrow, and it was much the
same story on the other streets along the route. The
motorcade is shown passing the premises where Carling and
Wright's radio and television business was beginning to benefit
from the increasing demand for television sets.*

Above: Purring silently past the Leeds General Infirmary, the first glimpse of the gleaming Rolls Royce limousine was the cue for deafening cheers from the thousands of people lining the route. Careful inspection of this picture reveals H.M. Queen Elizabeth and the Duke of Edinburgh beneath the wide perspex canopy in the rear of the car, the red and gold royal standard fluttering above their heads as it glides past the ecstatic throng. All the policemen, soldiers and St. John's Ambulance staff were immaculately turned-out, and the windows, balconies and canopies of the Brotherton Wing of the L.G.I were packed with enthusiastic cheering supporters. It was a day they would remember for the rest of their lives.

Top: *Nostalgia has much to do with proud moments. It would be difficult for Mr Lionel Jacobson, the Chairman of the most famous tailoring firm in Britain to think of a prouder moment than this one. The picture shows Mr Jacobson and H.M. Queen Elizabeth during her 1958 tour of the City. The Queen obviously enjoyed her visit to Burton's, the cheering beneath the low-ceiling in the factory was quite deafening, and applause broke out spontaneously as Her Majesty passed the eager workers. Burtons was established in Sheffield in 1900 with capital of £100. A modest Leeds factory began work before the First World War but it was after the war that the huge 100 acre site at Hudson Road was completed. Eventually there would be a workforce of 16,000 making quality tailored products on this site, supplying hundreds of Burtons shops throughout Britain and beyond.*

Part of H.M. Queen's visit to Leeds in 1958 involved inspecting the Guard of Honour on the forecourt of the Town Hall. Thousands of people lined the streets and several hundred patients and staff at the Leeds General Infirmary sought every possible vantage point from which to secure the best view of the proceedings. There was considerable excitement in Leeds on the day of the visit. Council workmen were on the streets from just after dawn to ensure that they were free from litter. People began to arrive from about 8.00 a.m in order to find a front row spot along the route, many equipped with sandwiches and flasks to sustain them during the wait.

What a great advert for the Boar Lane branch of Granada T.V! A group of around 20 men are transfixed by a programme on the sets in the window, despite the drizzle and the difficulties involved in peering over the shoulder of the strangers in front. Were we present we would have heard encouraging "oo's", "get it in there's" and "go-on lad's" - for the crowd was watching the exciting 1966 World Cup Final live from Wembley. Television has changed all our lives since it started to become available and popular from the 1950s. The Coronation in 1953 and coverage of State events and major sporting occasions greatly stimulated demand for sets. There were casualties of course, cinema-going was hit hardest and many previously popular cinema venues either closed or became bingo halls. Colour television was available on the B.B.C and I.T.V from 1969, just in time to watch Neil Armstrong take his first steps on the moon, Concorde make her maiden flight, and the QE2 set off on her maiden voyage.

Bottom: A scene from the Ostler's Arms, where the landlord displayed the front page from the *Evening News* each day out of respect for his journalistic clients who were known to spend much of their time here. This photograph dates from May 2nd 1962 and we can see that the big story of the day was the threat of a 4d per gallon price increase on petrol. At the time there were about 5 million private cars on Britain's roads - around a quarter of the number in the late 1990s. It is known that lunchtime and after-work drinking was a popular pastime among those involved with the newspaper business at the time. An arduous but apparently essential aspect of a journalists job.

Below: One of Leeds United's most successful and best-loved personalities was the multi-talented Billy Bremner. His long association with the club, his sense of loyalty, commitment and fair play won him a special place in the hearts of Leeds people. Even those not interested in the game recognised his rare qualities and standing as a sporting example to others. His premature passing led to a tremendous outpouring of grief among fans and ordinary people which is normally reserved for 'one of our own.' He is sadly missed.

Leeds United fans of all ages gather in admiration of their idols, Jack Charlton and Norman Hunter, outside the Civic Hall. The year was 1966, and the players were enjoying an even greater degree of stardom after their part in the England team's World Cup success in the final against West Germany. The team, captained by Bobby Moore had beaten the 1954 World Cup winners by 4 goals to 2. Geoff Hurst scored two goals in extra time to complete his hat-trick. He had been selected in preference to the prolific goal scorer Jimmy Greaves in a controversial decision by the England manager Alf Ramsey.

Leeds Hospital Fund - the unsung hero of local healthcare

In 1887, Mr Fred R Spark JP founded the Leeds & District Workpeople's Hospital Fund. Calling the leaders of the different trade unions and friendly societies together, he determined to approach all those in the workshops of Leeds and obtain from them weekly subscriptions. The first meeting was held in the Co-operative Hall, when a general committee was elected.

The first General Meeting was held in the Mayor's Rooms at the Town Hall, and, as public interest increased, sub-committees were formed in the various wards of Leeds.

The Fund was to be for the purpose of financing local hospitals, chiefly Leeds General Infirmary. In those days hospitals relied on donations for their continued existence and needed some form of regular and sustained income. The voluntary subscription was 1d a week and in the first year it yielded £1,883.

By 1913 when the National Insurance Scheme was inaugurated the Fund had grown to £13,226 annually and was too well established to be affected. In 1919 the subscription was increased to 2d, and again in 1942 to 3d, where it remained for a number of years. In 1947, the last full year before the inception of the new National Health Act, income reached an all time record of £172,000.

Substantial amounts of this money had been raised by special efforts, a significant one being the annual Bramley Carnival. Another was the Bank Holiday Gala in Roundhay Park, the last of these in 1939 raising £41,295. By this time the Fund had handed over almost £2 million to Leeds General Infirmary and other local hospitals. To celebrate its Golden Jubilee in 1937 a special gift

was made to LGI for the dedication of a ward that was named after the Fund.

The introduction of the National Health Service led to a depressing fall in income for the Fund from £172,000 to £105,000. It responded with a scheme that would provide supplementary benefits to the subscriber and the income from the Reserve Fund was made available for several charitable disbursements.

After negotiations with the Inland Revenue it was agreed that this reserve fund, used for charity and never for profit, should be exempt from income tax. So, charitable organisations within the city were helped without any call on the weekly subscriptions of members. At Christmas the Fund provided special food in the hospitals as well as decorations in the wards and presents for patients. The orthopaedic hospital at Thorp Arch was provided with a hydro-therapy unit to treat polio victims. Wharfdale Children's Hospital was given a 'Talkie-film projector', a record player and a

Above: One of the Leeds Hospital Fund's buses taking convalescent patients to Ilkley.
Facing page, top left: Fred Spark, who founded the Fund.
Facing page, top right: The executive committee from 1900 with Fred Spark in the centre with his wife.
Facing page, bottom: In this slightly later picture, Fred Spark can be seen in the centre with the umbrella.
Below: Some of the many vans and buses that the Fund used in the 1940s and 50s to provide chiropody services to the community.

television set. Equipment was also provided at St James', Killingbeck and Cookridge. Cash grants were given for cancer research, Care of Cripples, Guide Dogs for the Blind and many other deserving causes.

For members, paying their weekly contributions, cash grants were paid if they were admitted to hospital and grants were offered towards optical, dental, maternity, home help, surgical appliances and physiotherapy. The Fund was not private health insurance because the benefits it offered were ancillary and supplementary to the National Health Service.

The Fund had always been aware of the importance - and the expense - of convalescence. The first convalescent home owned and operated by the Fund was Springfield at Horsforth which had been opened in 1896 by the then Lord Mayor of Leeds, Alderman C F Tetley. There was great interest in the project and transport for visiting

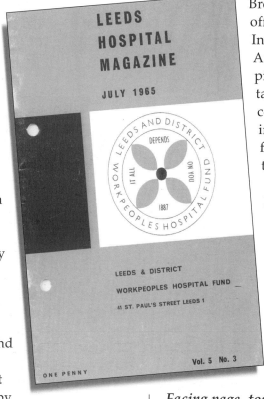

guests was arranged. Wagonettes went in procession from near Leeds Town Hall to Horsforth. Five hundred people watched the opening ceremony and Mr Walter Brown, a leading surgeon of the day, offered to be the acting consultant. In addition he persuaded his friend Archibald Ramsden to donate a piano for the use and entertainment of the patients. Other convalescent homes were opened in Ilkley until it became the fashion for the period of recovery to be spent at the coast.

In 1949 therefore the Fund's first seaside home was opened. The building in Bridlington, previously the Burlington Hotel, was

Left: A magazine issued by the Fund in 1965.
Top: This ambulance was given to the Leeds & District branch of the Infantile Paralysis Fellowship by the Fund in 1953.
Facing page, top: One of the many Leeds Hospital Fund vans providing chiropody services.
Facing page, bottom: The headquarters were opened in November 1955 by the Lord Mayor of Leeds, Sir James Croysdale.

attract the conva-
lescent workers who
might benefit from a
stay at Springfield.

In 1986 many of the
rules of the Home
were relaxed, and
room facilities were
provided where
patients could make
tea and coffee in their
rooms. A bar was
provided for relaxed
evenings and the take-
up improved.

By 1955 the office
premises in Park
Square, Leeds, had
become totally inade-
quate and organisation

renamed Springfield and adapted for use in men's
convalescence. When it proved very popular it
was decided to provide a women's seaside home.
The Manor Hotel, also in Bridlington, was bought.
It was opened in 1953 by Viscountess Swinton.

The architect for the project was Mr William
Backhouse.

The years between 1971 and 1985 saw a great
social change in the holiday habits of contributors.
Many were spending their holidays abroad. If
they stayed in this
country the standard
they demanded from
their hotel was very
high. This change had
an adverse effect on
the number and age
group of contributors
applying for convales-
cence.

The original concept
of the Fund's Homes
had been to provide
recuperative convales-
cence so that workers
could return to work
fully fit after illness or
accident. This was not
happening, so several
alterations were made
in an attempt to

was in danger of becoming chaotic. Office accommodation was at a premium and obtaining
building licenses was far from easy. It was
considered wiser to purchase a building suitable
for conversion than to attempt to rent large
premises, even if they could be found. Needing a
site as close as possible to the city centre, the
management chose the building at 41 St Paul's
Street, paying £6,850 in 1950. The Fund's archi-
tects faced many problems and it was decided to
reduce the building to a shell and reconstruct it
throughout.

Fund. In 1968, therefore, the Executive Committee began periodically adjusting its rates and benefits. It began in that year by a further increase of the rate to 6d. In 1970 it became a shilling.

Because of the value of the benefits being offered there was an increasing interest by the clerical staffs of firms and it was because of this wider implication that the name of the Fund was changed, missing out 'Workpeople's', to 'Leeds & District Hospital Fund'.

In 1972 the Fund acted as host to the national conference of

In 1965 the weekly subscription for all workers was increased to 4d, though pensioners continued to pay at the old rate. However, the mid sixties was the beginning of a period of inflation in this country which very quickly had the effect of reducing the value of the benefits offered by the

the British Hospitals Contributory Schemes Association. The latter association had been formed in 1948 as a national body to meet and consider ways of increasing the activities of contributory schemes and improving benefits offered to contributors.

In 1973, after the decimalisation of the currency, the rate of contributions was increased to 10p with a reduced rate of 6p for non-working pensioners. 1977 brought a further increase to 15p.

The increase in the Fund's activities made it essential that reserves were built up to meet any period of loss of revenue. Therefore, in 1978, a stockbroker was engaged to advise on the investment of the Fund's monies. In 1980 the rate was increased to 30p.

As interest in the Fund extended beyond the immediate vicinity of Leeds, the Executive Committee decided to take out of its title the words '& District'. In 1981 the necessary legal steps were taken to change the name of the Fund to 'Leeds Hospital Fund Limited'.

As there were now over 200,000 contributors to the Fund, it became vital for the administration record keeping to be streamlined. In the same year, 1981, therefore, a computer was installed to deal efficiently with the ever-increasing workload.

In 1983 the rate was increased to 50p. Four years later, however, the maternity grant was doubled, from £30 to £60, without any increase in contributions.

Above: Viewing of some of the equipment donated to local hospitals. Facing page, top: The official opening of the Manor Convalescent home. Facing page, bottom: A selection of Leeds Hospital Fund trophies. Right: A generous donation made to the Lineham Farm Appeal by the Charitable Trust of Leeds Hospital Fund.

Fund is open to all aged 17 to 61, either through direct contributions or payroll deduction. The Fund has developed a network of companies throughout the UK who support it in offering payroll deduction facilities to their staff and enable the Fund to continue to offer the quality of product it has become known for.

In line with tradition the Fund still operates a convalescent home in Bridlington which was refurbished in 1992 to hotel standards. All contributors in need of convalescence, following hospitalisation or illness are welcome and it provides a restful atmosphere for employees hoping to make a speedy recovery and return to work.
The Fund's links with the community continue to be of great importance, and its Charitable Trust, headed by its Chairman, Mrs. Pam Dobson, continues to work relentlessly to this end. In 1997 a sum in excess of half a million pounds was issued through specific grants and donations to hospitals and local charities.

A special centenary gift of £10,000 each was given to the Leeds Western Health Authority and the Leeds Eastern Health Authority to acknowledge the close links which exist between the Fund and the local hospitals and have done for more than a hundred years.

The Fund continues today in the same traditions. The company is non profit making and returns virtually all its contributory income, less administrative costs, back to its contributors in the form of benefits. In 1997 payouts to contributors topped £16.5 million, making it the UK's third largest cash plan.

In January 1998 the Fund launched a new streamlined package of cash benefits - the 'LHF Healthplan'. This package provides low cost healthcare for all the family in the form of actual cash towards a wide range of treatments - and in line with current trends in medicine includes some alternative therapies. Enrolment into the

Today the Fund continues to focus on its contributors, providing an efficient, cost effective service with the emphasis on customer care.

Above: Springfield Convalescent Home.
Below: Members of the current Board led by (third from right) Mr T. Hardy BEM in his fourth year as Chairman.

Around the City centre

A wealth of information is contained in this picture from 1929. City Square is shown from the direction of Aire Street. The War Memorial, Post Office Road, Wellington Street, Park Row and Boar Lane are all featured in this inspiring picture. One of the first things to strike us is the number of horse-drawn vehicles in the scene. Several of these have large barrels on the back of them. Many firms relied upon this method of distribution for their products right up until the 1940s. Two trams in the photograph carry prominent advertisements for *Melbourne Ales.*

Right: The Headrow and the recently-opened Lewis's store can be seen in this picture which was taken looking from Albion Street. It dates from July 1934 and also features the Central Garage Company on the left of the photograph with an advertising slogan "Austin, Britain's dependable cars" on the wall. During the year this picture was taken a number of inventions and innovations were introduced which would affect the lives of ordinary people. 'Cats Eyes' were invented by Percy Shaw in nearby Halifax, making a major contribution to road safety and making the shrewd Yorkshireman a millionaire. In the U.S.A the cheeseburger was invented by Carl Kaelen at his restaurant in Kentucky. Nearer home, the Mersey tunnel was opened in 1934 by H.M. King George V. It was, at the time, the longest underwater tunnel in the world.

This photograph of The Headrow was taken in may 1940, when attention was firmly focused on the war. The scene is dominated by the imposing, soot-stained building which houses the Public Art Gallery and Library. Careful scrutiny reveals evidence of wartime preparations. Sandbags can be seen along the wall and the glass bowls have been removed from the tall street lamps along Centenary Street. Some of the motors in the picture have had white lines painted on their mudguards and bumpers to aid visibility in the blackout, which it didn't much.

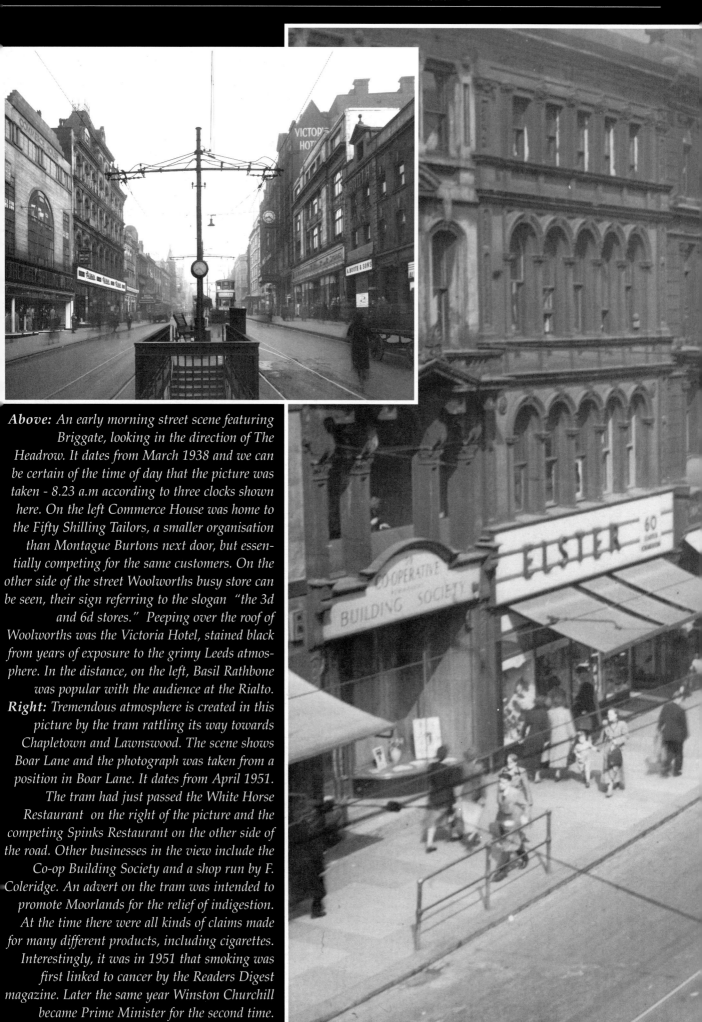

Above: *An early morning street scene featuring Briggate, looking in the direction of The Headrow. It dates from March 1938 and we can be certain of the time of day that the picture was taken - 8.23 a.m according to three clocks shown here. On the left Commerce House was home to the Fifty Shilling Tailors, a smaller organisation than Montague Burtons next door, but essentially competing for the same customers. On the other side of the street Woolworths busy store can be seen, their sign referring to the slogan "the 3d and 6d stores." Peeping over the roof of Woolworths was the Victoria Hotel, stained black from years of exposure to the grimy Leeds atmosphere. In the distance, on the left, Basil Rathbone was popular with the audience at the Rialto.*

Right: *Tremendous atmosphere is created in this picture by the tram rattling its way towards Chapletown and Lawnswood. The scene shows Boar Lane and the photograph was taken from a position in Boar Lane. It dates from April 1951. The tram had just passed the White Horse Restaurant on the right of the picture and the competing Spinks Restaurant on the other side of the road. Other businesses in the view include the Co-op Building Society and a shop run by F. Coleridge. An advert on the tram was intended to promote Moorlands for the relief of indigestion. At the time there were all kinds of claims made for many different products, including cigarettes. Interestingly, it was in 1951 that smoking was first linked to cancer by the Readers Digest magazine. Later the same year Winston Churchill became Prime Minister for the second time.*

The photographer was standing on Duncan Street when he took this picture, looking west along Boar Lane across Briggate. The picture dates from early in 1943, a time when the thoughts of most people were still firmly fixed on the war and the streets were still criss-crossed overhead by miles of cable for the tram system. The large, boldly-signed shop to the right, on the corner of Briggate, was Saxone Shoes. It faced the equally-brash Fifty Shilling Taylors store across the way and each was part of a growing national chain of similar branches serving the needs of well dressed people in the first half of the twentieth century. Approaching the camera is a friendly-faced Bedford lorry. Careful scrutiny reveals that it was part of the fleet of trucks used by Robertsons to take their delightful 'Golden Shred' marmalade to eager customers throughout the district and beyond. Some white markings on the kerbs and street furniture are clues to the blackout regulations which caused more than their fair share of minor (and not so minor) accidents.

Above: Standing at the junction of The Headrow and Briggate, looking along lower Headrow towards Eastgate, resulted this view from 1944. The picture is dominated by the Odeon cinema which was showing *The Story of Bernadette* at the time. The classic movie starred Charles Bickford and Jennifer Jones and was billed as the "Big Screen's Immortal Triumph" on the fascia signs outside the cinema. Cobbled roads were still in evidence around Leeds at this time. Tarmac was first laid around 1910 but it was not commonly used until the 1920s. This picture was taken late in 1944 as the Second World War was drawing to a close. Just a few weeks earlier Field Marshal Erwin Rommel had committed suicide after a plot to assassinate Hitler was exposed.

Left: It is obvious to anyone from the clues contained within this picture that it dates from wartime. We know from a note on the reverse of the print that it was taken in October 1944. Large water tanks line The Headrow, ready to be used if the mains water supply was damaged by bombing and essential for the fire fighters tackling any blaze started by enemy attack. Still, by the time this picture was taken the threat posed by the Nazis was beginning to recede. The D-Day landings had taken place some four months earlier. A month after the picture was taken the blackout was lifted in London after five long years. Victory was on the horizon.

Bottom: This is how the north side of Boar Lane looked in 1948. The tall, dignified but extremely grimy exterior of Holy Trinity Church dominates the picture and the clock on the building is showing 'noon.' In the shadow of the church the costumiers business operated by J.Jones can be seen, and the other side of the imposing building the C&A department store has drawn all the shades to protect the goods in their window. Interestingly, a faded sign on the fascia of C&A's can be seen which goes back to the days when the full name of the business was 'C&A Modes.' Tramlines and cars from the period complete the scene for us.

Below: The South West side of The Headrow is featured in this picture, at the junction of Albion Street. The dyers and cleaners operated by Martins can be seen on the right, below the offices where scores of young ladies worked away in the clerical department of the Leeds and Holbeck Building Society. These ladies may have taken advantage of the offer in Martin's window which read "silk or nylon stockings repaired for 6d."

Their fathers may have been more interested in the adjacent notice describing the shop as the "Leeds broken pipe mender." The picture was taken in May 1951, an era during which the scale of criminal activity was rather different to the one we face today. Clear evidence of this comes in the form of the billboard beside the newspaper vendor in this picture. The bill reads *'Leeds van with load of sweets stolen.'* The story would struggle to get *into* the papers today, let alone be featured on the newsbills.

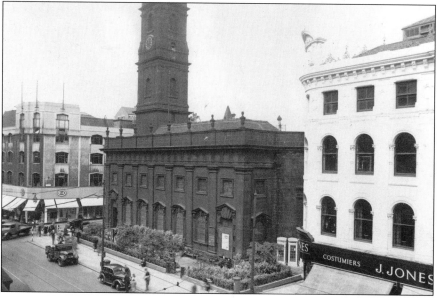

The North West side of Briggate as it appeared in February 1944 is featured here. The substantial Rothwell's furniture store is shown on the right of the picture and the sign for Parkers Hotel dominates the foreground. The minds of the handful of passers-by would have been dominated by thoughts of wartime, though they would have been well aware that the conflict was drawing to a positive conclusion by this time. It was estimated that around 100,000 Leeds men and 10,000 local women served in the Second World War and for every person away at the front there were dozens of fretting relatives thinking about them at home.

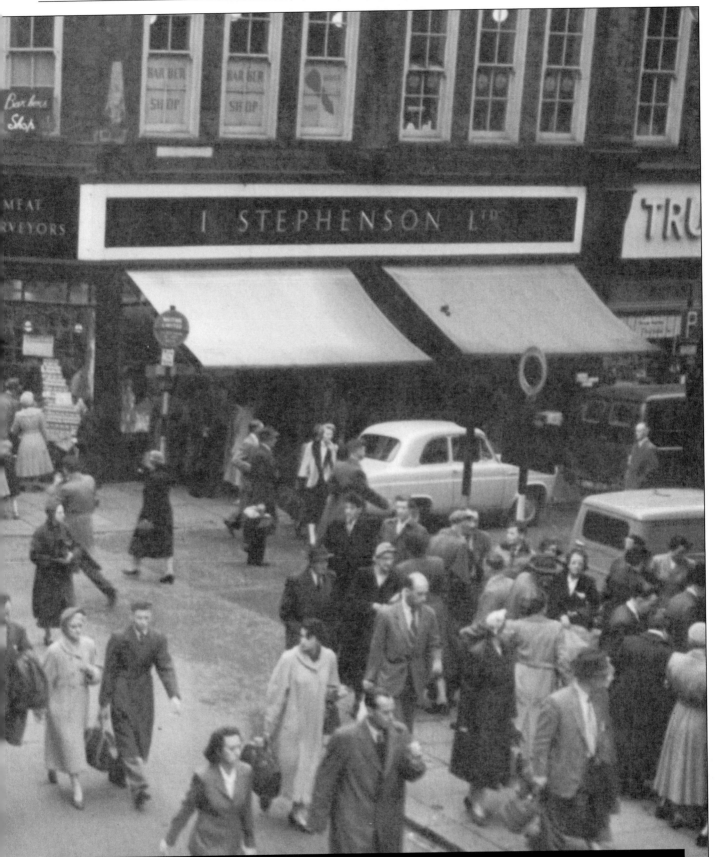

The Kirkgate area of Leeds is shown as it looked during the mid-1950s. As you would expect, the street is crowded with people hurrying along the pavements and spilling over onto the narrow roadway as a consequence of the sheer volume of numbers. By the time this picture had been taken many of the citizens of Leeds were beginning to enjoy af higher standard of living than had been the case in the first years after the end of the war. The conflict had left Britain's economy in bad shape, with over £3000 million of overseas debt and many factories, ports and railways smashed by German bombs. The people shown here had lived through difficult times in the 'austerity' years but most of them were about to experience the benefit of a period of economic prosperity. Famously, they would be told by Harold Macmillan in 1957 that 'You've never had it so good.'

Above: The corner of Mill Hill and Boar Lane is dominated by the *Griffin Hotel*, the ornate and imposing bar, restaurant and hotel known and loved by so many over the years. The kiosk on the corner provided hotel guests, passers-by and bar customers with all the news and sports results they could bear in the form of daily newspapers. This was 1947, a time of rationing, cut-backs and austerity, a year which saw the launch of the first Polaroid camera, the opening of Britain's first atomic reactor (at Harwell, Oxfordshire) and the death of the founder of the Ford Motor Company, Henry Ford.

This delightful scene dates from 1955 and features City Square with the Norwich Union offices, Barclays Bank and the Post Office clearly in view. The centrepiece of the picture is the statue of the Black Prince which had marked the spot since 1903 when this picture was taken. The City Square was created at the turn of the century and has provided a 'first impression of Leeds' for millions of incoming railway travellers for almost a century. A sign on Mill Hill Chapel (consecrated in 1848) appeals for £40,000 for urgently needed repairs and many, mainly elderly people take advantage of the seats around the Black Prince to recharge their batteries in the May sunshine. In the distance a well-stacked coal wagon operated by Leeds Co-op is slowly making its way around the traffic island, its labouring engine would have provided competition for the quiet conversation around the statue.

Only a few decades after it was completed, the Queen's Hotel had taken on a rather grimy appearance which did not do justice to its imposing architectural style or its position overlooking the prestigious City Square. This picture was taken in the 1950s, clear evidence coming in the shape of the motorcars in the background on the right hand side of the shot. There was a tram between the position of the photographer and the Leeds City Railway Station and shelters on the traffic island provided at least a little shelter for those waiting for their transport home.

Above: The stylish *Clock Cinema* provided entertainment for all ages at this prominent position in Harehills. Careful inspection reveals a gas lamp on the right of the photograph and character is generated by the 1930s saloon parked near the window cleaner's barrow. The window cleaner is perched precariously some 25 feet up the building, playing his part in making sure that everything was spick and span for the cinema's customers. They say that most things come and go and this is certainly true in the world of cinema. The period between 1960 and the mid 1970s saw many cinemas either close down completely or be converted into bingo halls. The cause was attributed to the massive increase in television ownership. Recent times have seen a welcome resurgence in the popularity of cinema going, but during quieter times many fine old cinema buildings were pulled down. Thankfully the Clock Ciinema remained intact, after finding a useful role as the base for a successful electrical retailer.

Below: The Kingsway Cinema along Harrogate Road will remembered by thousands of film goers in the district. It opened in June 1937 and was designed by James Brodie of nearby Pudsey. Perhaps surprisingly, its life as a cinema lasted little over twenty years. It closed in 1959 and re-opened in September that year as the New Vilna Synagogue.

A big hole was all that remained of the Royal Exchange Building which had looked out across City Square for 92 years. Passers-by were performing the age old ritual of standing around, looking gormless and staring into the void. This scene was recorded for us in 1964 and is actually *two* photographs, taken within a moment of each other to create the wide-angle effect. The Queen's Hotel is on the left of course, with the imposing dark mass of the Post Office in front of the camera. The Black Prince looks rather pleased with himself with shoulders back and a jaunty pose. Keen eyes may be able to make out the point-duty police officer standing on a tiny platform in the foreground. Before 'statistics' were invented *Point Duty* was once a major part of the policeman's role.

Right: A 1950s scene showing the West Bar area at the end of Boar Lane. Trams add a sense of character to the photograph, as do the passers-by in their distinctive 1950s clothing. The Midland Bank's curved and very ornate facade was intended to project an image of wealth and stability - for obvious reasons. Much more fun was on offer a hundred yards further along the street in the *Griffin Hotel. Boots* the chemists had a large store on the corner opposite the Griffin but it was pulled down within a decade or so of this photograph being taken.

It was a case of 'all change' in City Square when this scene was recorded. The early 1960s motorcars are a dead giveaway to the date from which the picture originates and the clock on the old Post Office building tells us that it was 2.45 p.m. The Post Office was opened in 1898 having taken almost two years to construct. The statue of the Black Prince is almost obscured from view by a lamp post. To the right of the very substantial Post Office was the curved facade of the Norwich Union Building with Barclays Bank beneath it. This property would be pulled down quite soon after this picture was taken in order to make way for a modern structure of concrete, steel and glass. This was entirely in-keeping with the tastes and thinking of the time, but fashions soon changed and it too was demolished and replaced with a breathtaking modern design.

On the home front

This aerial view of the Quarry Hill Flats can rightly be described as breathtaking. The sheer scale of the development as seen from the air is awe-inspiring, we can only guess at the incredible volumes of steel and concrete used in the construction of the dwellings which would attract so much controversy in later years. The modern, sweeping lines of the flats development created a sharp contrast to some of the dark, traditional buildings which surrounded it. Work at approaching the final stages when the picture was taken; use of a strong magnifying glass reveals three trams running along their track at the bottom left of the scene. The gas holder on the edge of the flats development looks out of place and potentially catastrophic when we consider the tons of German bombs which would be dropped in the city within the next decade.

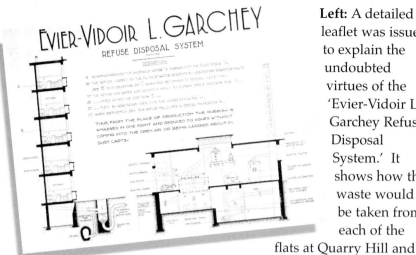

Left: A detailed leaflet was issued to explain the undoubted virtues of the 'Evier-Vidoir L. Garchey Refuse Disposal System.' It shows how the waste would be taken from each of the flats at Quarry Hill and whisked away to the 'disposal station.' The obvious advantages were that the system meant allowed the immediate disposal of household waste without the need for dustbins which might attract flies and pests. Also, of course, there was no requirement for men to empty the bins - an unenviable task in a large development of flats. One added bonus was that much of the waste could be burned, and this provided a source of steam that could be used in the communal laundry. A 125ft chimney carried the remaining smoke away from the complex.

Below: This tidy living room could be found in one of the flats at Quarry Hill. There is everything you could have wished for in terms of home comforts - but no T.V. yet, for this was the 1950s. Even by this time there were reports that *some* residents at the flats were unhappy with certain aspects of life there. The construction work had set off with high hopes but the war had caused delays to some aspects of the project whilst some elements were abandoned altogether. Newspaper reports mentioned peeling paint and defective lifts among the complaints, as well as the closure of the British Restaurant (in March 1949) and the Council's failure to maintain safe playing areas for the children. Two full-time wardens had been employed on the estate from the 1940s but it is said that their roles were not clearly enough defined for them to be totally effective.

This picture shows a lady resident at Quarry Hill Flats about to demonstrate the effectiveness of the waste disposal system which was built into her kitchen. The waste was carried away to a central incinerator which produced the steam used in the communal laundry area. Smoke was carried away from the flats by a 125ft chimney. The automated waste disposal system was operational from November 1939. Of the 938 dwellings 80 were of the 2 bedroom variety, 413 had 3 bedrooms, 381 had 4, 22 had 5 and 42 had 6 rooms. Rents at the flats in 1939 varied from 10s 10d (about 54p) to 18s 10d (about 94p) per week.

A sea of faces greeted the photographer when he arrived to take this picture at Quarry Hill's annual carnival in 1951. The level of excitement is visible on the faces of the children shown here. And no wonder, for the event would have been looked-forward to by all of them for many months. Quarry Hill Carnival was taken seriously by grown-ups too, including those who lived outside the flat-dwelling community. Indeed, the Lord Mayor of Leeds, Lieutenant Colonel F. Eric Tetley opened the event and his wife crowned the new Carnival Queen. Among the events designed to entertain the crowds were a Bonny Baby competition, a parade of 20 decorated vehicles and a concert performed by local children at night.

Above: This picture shows the Quarry Hill Flats as bright as a new pin, complete with the new bus station just a short stroll away rom the revolutionary new living accommodation. Work on the flats had begun in 1934, only 5 years before this picture was taken. They were noted for many things, but initially two talking points were the luxury of electric lifts and the novel Garchy waterborne waste disposal system. In all there were 930 flats, constructed at a density of just 36 per acre allowing a feeling of openness which was the envy of people living in the crowded narrow streets in other parts of the city. The idea was that the open space could be used for gardens, bowling greens, tennis courts and playgrounds, though some of these facilities never actually saw the light of day. The onset of war put a stop to further building and development of the complex, and some would later say that this interruption led to the defects in the accommodation which led to its ultimate demise. By 1950 some 3500 people lived here, most with a pride and contentment in their homes which was quite exceptional for the day.

Right: This charming picture was taken in the mid-1950s at one of the annual Quarry Hill Carnivals. The three little lads were dressed in their Sunday best in order to perform Page-Boy duties for the *Miss Teenager* contest. At least one of them looks less than pleased with his forthcoming assignment, and no wonder. Times certainly have changed as far as fashion is concerned. Try getting your little lad to wear a jacket and trousers... let alone a tie!

Left: Life in the back-to-back houses in the Armley/Wortley district is featured in this provocative photograph from the mid 1960s. The street was known as "15th Avenue." Gas lamps still lit the uneven pavements (isn't it strange how the reproduction versions seen in posh gardens never look as authentic?) and the billowing washing would have been prepared without the aid of a washing machine inside the tiny brick houses. There was a constant battle against cold and damp in the winter months, and the rows of chimneys provided a grey backdrop when the residents had their coal fire lit. It wasn't all bad news however; many former residents recall the days when everyone knew and respected their neighbours (unlike today when many people know the characters on *Coronation Street* better than they know the folk next door) and burglary and muggings were as unusual as central heating.

Bird's eye view

Below: One of the largest and most ambitious civil engineering problems ever seen in the district, the Inner Ring Road cut a swathe through the city when it was constructed in 1966. The Clay Pit Lane area is featured and the picture gives a good impression of the scale of the undertaking and the disruption it caused to traders and travellers during the work. There was no disputing the need for a solution to the burgeoning congestion that was slowly choking the city centre. It was much the same story in every other town and city as the number of vehicles on the roads increased. In 1953 there had been one car on the road for every 24 people in Britain. By the mid-1960s this had risen to one in every 7 people. Road building had almost become a national obsession. Motorway building had started in 1958 and the first 75 mile stretch of Motorway, the M1 opened a year later. By the 1970s Britain had 750 miles of Motorway helping to take traffic away from the centre of cities like Leeds.

This late 1960s aerial view already shows Leeds as a modern go-ahead city. Within a year or two of the picture being taken the huge Quarry Hill Flats complex would be pulled down in the midst of considerable controversy. The new A64 taking traffic to York and the coast beyond runs diagonally from top to bottom on the left hand side of this picture. There is no evidence in this view of the tremendous volume of cars and trucks it would carry in later years. Virtually all the available space shown here was turned over to car parking, a sign of the times and a sign of things to come. It was usual for demolition sites to be used as temporary car parks at this time. 'Temporary' could mean a few months or a couple of years in the sixties and seventies.

A fine aerial view of the centre of Leeds shows the Quarry Hill Flats development at the top right of the picture and The Headrow running away from them to the left. The distinctive round roof of the Corn Exchange is present just below, and to the right of, the centre of the photograph. Many of the tightly-packed domestic and commercial properties shown here would be swept away in the redevelopment of the city centre.

A late 1950s view of the Quarry Hill Flats, the Bus Station and the market area. The distinctive long pitched roofs of the market building can be seen on the left of the picture, showing just what a large piece of land they occupy. Devastation was to strike in 1975 when a massive fire destroyed more than half of the structure. It was the largest fire that Leeds had endured for many decades. The flats at Quarry Hill dominate the picture. By this point in time they had been occupied for about twenty years and their inevitable, though regrettable, end was in sight.

Left: This aerial view of the centre of the city was taken in August 1968 from and aircraft flying at 1200 ft. The Headrow dissects the scene from top to bottom and the lower left hand corner of the picture is occupied by the Town Hall, Library and Museum. At the top of The Headrow the curved outline of Quarry Hill Flats can just be seen, in the top right hand corner of this picture. It is obvious from the photograph that the era of high-rise retail, office and residential buildings was upon us. There is a sharp contrast between the very modern concrete structures at the top left of the picture with the soot-stained older property bordering The Headrow. Our relatively clean air these days is generally taken for granted. Yet, as recently as the 1950s polluted air caused widespread bronchial problems and thousands of premature deaths throughout the country.

Above: At first glance there is nothing much unusual about this aerial photograph of the centre of the city. Closer inspection reveals that building work was actually taking place on several well-known structures at the time the picture was taken. This construction work was likely to be the reason that the photograph was commissioned. At the top of the picture one of the city's most ambitious projects was well underway. The Quarry Hill Flats were taking shape with all the steelwork in place and much of the pre-fabricated panels already secured. There was still some work being carried out on the roof of Lewis's store on The Headrow but the other large construction project shown is nearer the bottom left hand corner of the picture. The Brotherton Wing of the L.G.I was about half way through the building process. It stands near the Civic Hall which was opened by King George and Queen Mary in 1933. From all these clues it is believed that this splendid historical picture was taken in 1937.

Right: A number of interesting elements are contained in this late 1940s aerial view. We cannot fail to be struck by the blackened buildings and wonder at the damage the smoke and fumes must have done to our lungs at the time. The Headrow is shown running left to right with the Library and Museum clearly visible on the left. Further to the right the old H.Q of the Leeds Permanent Building Society can be seen. The centrepiece of the picture is the Peace Gardens on The Headrow complete with War Memorial. The Memorial itself features 'Winged Victory,' a female figure beneath repre-sents Peace. It had initially been positioned on a site at Cookridge Street, unveiled in October 1922 by Lord Lascelles. Leeds had lost an estimated 10,000 men during the Great War and the magnif-icent statue was designed as a focal point for the remembrance of the city's brave warriors. By 1937 the increasing number of vehicles using Cookridge Street made the location of the memorial inappro-priate. It was therefore moved to the more suitable position on The Headrow.

Left: A 1936 birds-eye view of City Square, the Queens Hotel and surrounding area. It is interesting to see just how bright the stonework of the new hotel is compared to the tarnished appearance it would take on just a couple of decades later. The picture was taken in ideal conditions affording a clear view of subtle details of the buildings shown. A good impression of the sheer size of Leeds Railway Station is given, along with the River Aire basin to the right of it. Pedestrians can be seen like ants walking along most of the streets and in particular in City Square. Some of them may have been walking towards the Post Office to the right of the square. It looks huge in this photograph. It is interesting to consider some of the events which would have been on the minds of the people on the streets, some 1200 feet below the photographer in 1936; they may have been aware that the B.B.C had launched the first regular television service in London, and they would have known for certain that Fred Perry had won the Men's Singles title in Wimbledon for the third year running. By the end of the year the biggest story of 1936 had broken - the abdication of King Edward VIII who gave up his crown for the love of American divorcee Wallis Simpson.

Above: There have been many changes to Wellington Street since this picture was taken. The number 15 tram bound for Whingate is shown in the centre of the scene, surrounded by curvaceous motor saloons which typified the mid 1950s period of the picture. James Hare's serge manufacturing business is featured opposite the position of the cameraman and the premises of Falks the electrical suppliers is shown further towards the city centre. The whole street looks blackened by years of exposure to the emissions of thousands of local chimneys. Nobody could fail to see the publicity material for Mackeson's stout on the advertising hoarding and on the tramcar.

Right: This picture was taken in March 1956 and features Cookridge Street. Trams could still be seen on the streets of Leeds at the time and this picture is dominated by the lovely period motorcars casually parked on the side of what was to become a very busy thoroughfare. 'Yellow Lines' would change all that, the first ones being introduced in June 1958. Motoring became popular again during the 1950s. Petrol rationing had ended in May 1950 and all the major manufacturers competed with each other to bring out exciting new models to satisfy the demand. It was the age of the Consul and the Zephyr - and by the end of the decade the Mini was born.

On the move

It is just possible to make out the edge of the Burton's building on the left of this picture. The association that Burtons has had with the City of Leeds is well documented. The company made a tremendous fortune from their ability to make and sell good value gents clothing, and eventually boasted similar distinctive stores in the hub of almost every town of note in the U.K. The photograph was taken in July 1956 and is interesting for the fact that it features a bus and a tram about to cross each other along Lower Briggate. The number 10 bus was bound for Wakefield and Kettlethorpe and shown about to pass a young man riding a large British (of course) motorcycle. The biker was not wearing a helmet - it would be another two decades before common sense became compulsory. Keen eyes may be able to make out the sign marking the location of the Royal Hotel across the road.

Above: In the days before Sky T.V local football supporters would often travel to the game by tram. Special tramcars like these would usually be laid on to cater for the demand. This picture shows a number of (mainly) men and boys on their way to see Leeds United playing at Elland Road in April 1955. A significant number of fans had elected to walk to the match. This is a good picture of a crowded tram because it shows how tightly packed in the passengers were in the cramped cabin. Small cardboard advertisements in the windows of the trams promote awareness of a forthcoming *Chipperfields Circus* and various theatre and film shows. Larger adverts on the outside of the trams urge us to sample *Capstan* cigarettes and *Orme's* best boiled sweets.

Above: This view of Oakwood features Barkers Garage as it appeared in July 1961. They sold the popular Morris, Riley and M.G marques among others. The picture was taken to record the procession of motor vehicles at the Childrens' Day Festival. The two single-deck buses in the foreground were of the A.E.C Reliance type, built around 1959. Behind the buses a loudspeaker van based on a Bedford can be seen making its way up the hill, followed by a lorry owned by R.J. Gaunt Ltd. with a display based upon 'The Three Little Pigs' on its flat-backed body.

Top: Happy memories of rides on rattling single-deckers will be prompted by this picture. The bus in question was made by A.E.C in 1954 and the picture dates from August 1959. The vehicle was easing itself into traffic at the junction of Stainbeck Road and Meanwood Road, part of the number 45 service for Meanwood, Headingley and Kirkstall. The Yorkshire Penny Bank occupied the corner property behind the bus with G. Franks Sweets and Chocolates shop to the left of it. Further along was Charles' the hairdresser. The 1950 motors are capable of bringing back memories too; a *Ford,* a *Morris* and a *Standard* can be seen on the right of the picture.

The number 14 bus stands at the Kirkgate Corn
Exchange Island against the impressive backdrop of the
Leeds City Market building. The market was opened in
1904 to supersede the former Kirkgate Market. The tram
stand for the number 8 service to Elland Road can be
seen in the foreground. It was removed from this spot
shortly after the picture was taken. This photograph was
taken in June 1955.

Above: There was drama at Yeadon Airport in February 1965 when this unfortunate British Midland *Dakota* aircraft ran off the end of the runway and buried itself in a muddy bank. The accident was caused by heavy rain which reduced the grip of the tyres under braking, with the result that the aircraft would not stop within the length of the runway. Nobody was seriously injured and most were able to make the muddy trek to back to the airport buildings with the minimum of assistance. Several workers were busy on a project to extend the runway when the accident happened. Thankfully one of them had noticed the fast-approaching Dakota and all made a safe, but hasty exit from the scene. Less than six months after this picture was taken a De Havilland Trident of BEA made the first ever 'automatic landing' at London's Heathrow Airport.

Left: Trams, buses and lorries squeeze through the narrow streets of Leeds en-route to various destinations. It is hard to believe that vehicles on long journeys had to pass through the centre of virtually every town and city along the way in the days before ring roads and motorways. In the 1960s and 1970s the planners began separating local traffic from the long distance motors which had no need to pass through our central shopping and business areas - and what a difference that made. The lorry at the bottom right of the picture is one of thousands of drab olive-green British Road Services trucks which had a charmed, government-protected existence at a time when independent transport operators were severely restricted. The double decker bus (number 54) shown here passing Jacomelli's Restaurant was taking weary shoppers to Bramley. This picture of Boar Lane was taken in April 1954 looking towards City Square.

Shopping Spree

Kirkgate on a busy shopping day. A wealth of information is contained in the picture which was taken in July 1956 and looks in the direction of Briggate. It is another scene which reminds us of the less rigorous parking restrictions which prevailed during the 1950s. It wouldn't last too long however, as by the 1960s city-centre congestion and the rapidly growing number of cars on the roads would result in the introduction of parking meters. They were first seen on the streets of Leeds in April 1964 and the first charge was 6d.

Memories of city centre shopping trips are certain to be prompted by this photograph. It features Lands Lane with the shops along the east side in view as the photographer points his device towards the north. Thornton's Arcade is prominent with the zebra crossing immediately in front of it. There were no parking restrictions here - or if there were they were being ignored by the curvaceous saloons parked along the street.

People who shopped here at the time would remember some of the retailers visible here - Ross Furs (who were advertising a five shillings in the pound discount sale at the time) and T. Mabane & Sons who were noted for their shoes and luggage. Beyond Mabane's, on the right, Swan Street could be found.

Top: A view looking West along The Headrow with Lewis's and the Paramount Cafe and Tea Room on the right hand side of the street. Lewis's were helping with a £250,000 appeal fund for the Leeds General Infirmary. The sign was intended to promote interest in the campaign by letting shoppers see how much progress had been made towards the target. What *gets measured gets done* and all that. *Bolero* was showing at the Paramount with George Raft and Carole Lombard. Yet another sign, this time on the lamp post in the middle of the road, was put there by the R.A.C and points in the direction of the Test Match. The photograph was taken in 1934.

Below: Lewis's store as it appeared in March 1949 with Headrow shoppers dodging the cars in order to get to the dominant local landmark in *state of the art* retailing. The store had first began trading from this spot in the mid 1930s and the quality and range of products on offer drew shoppers from miles around. Of course, at the time this picture was taken there were still restrictions on the goods available because of the rationing which still applied to many products. Rationing did not end completely in Britain until 1954, but clothes rationing ended just a month before this picture was taken, in February 1949. There are at least four fur coats in the picture. They give the wrong impression of the economic conditions which prevailed at the time as the country struggled to rebuild its economy. Before the end of 1949 the economic crisis was such that the Pound had to be devalued by 30%.

Above: The east side of Briggate as it appeared to passers-by in the closing years of the war. You would be hard pressed to find a more imposing sign than the one denoting the location of the Cash Clothing Company and its proud boast to be 'the largest clothiers in the world.' One of the windows in the shop was turned over to a wartime display with a large map of Europe. A caption on the map reads 'Russia: reconstruction begins.' To the right of the Cash Clothing Company was the Stylo boot and shoe company. Their slogan was 'Step In - and Step Out in Style.' Further right was the narrow entrance to the Bay Horse Hotel. Dixons, where service was available 'with a smile,' (a novel idea taken up by most shops in days gone by) were having their windows cleaned by the Central Window Cleaning Co. of Leeds, the ladders for the job being transported there on a large hand cart.

It was early in July 1956 when the photographer recorded this view. The location was Lands Lane in Leeds, looking south from The Headrow. The area is characteristically busy, shoppers drawn to the unrepeatable offers at Campbells, The Benefit Footwear shop and the other businesses on the parade. Notice the News van on the right of the picture, squeezing through the crowded streets to make its urgent deliveries. We can just make out two shiny black Rolls Royce's approaching the camera through the sea of single-minded shoppers. The purpose of the limousine's journey is not clear. Could they have been transporting celebrities from the Theatre Royal? - or were they part of a diverted funeral procession? - we may never know.

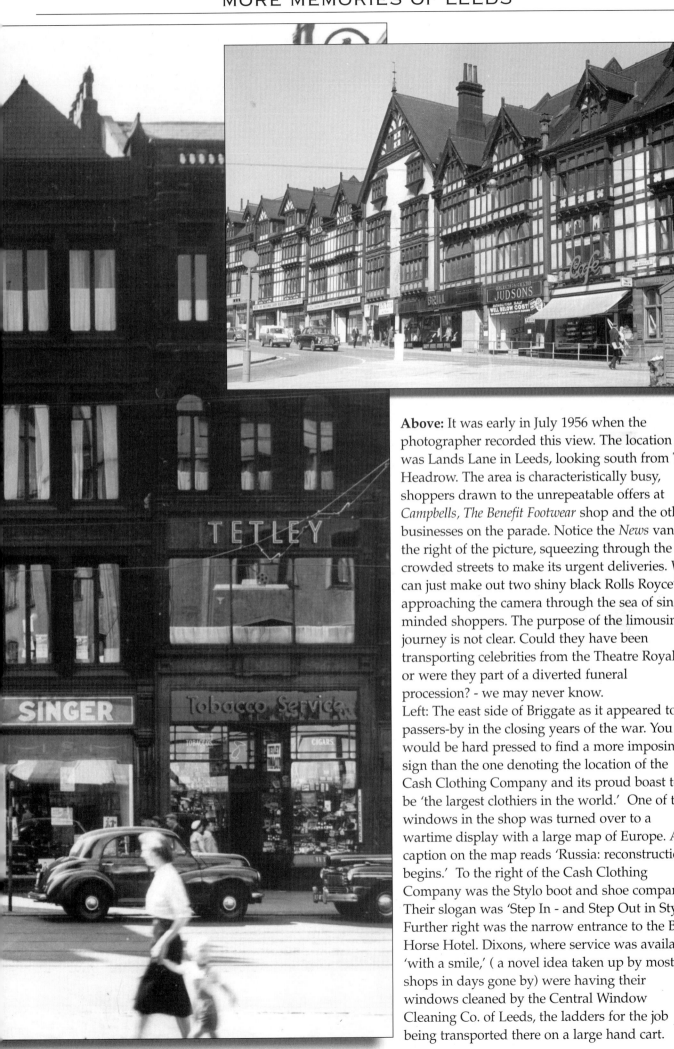

Above: It was early in July 1956 when the photographer recorded this view. The location was Lands Lane in Leeds, looking south from The Headrow. The area is characteristically busy, shoppers drawn to the unrepeatable offers at *Campbells, The Benefit Footwear* shop and the other businesses on the parade. Notice the *News* van on the right of the picture, squeezing through the crowded streets to make its urgent deliveries. We can just make out two shiny black Rolls Royce's approaching the camera through the sea of single-minded shoppers. The purpose of the limousine's journey is not clear. Could they have been transporting celebrities from the Theatre Royal? - or were they part of a diverted funeral procession? - we may never know.

Left: The east side of Briggate as it appeared to passers-by in the closing years of the war. You would be hard pressed to find a more imposing sign than the one denoting the location of the Cash Clothing Company and its proud boast to be 'the largest clothiers in the world.' One of the windows in the shop was turned over to a wartime display with a large map of Europe. A caption on the map reads 'Russia: reconstruction begins.' To the right of the Cash Clothing Company was the Stylo boot and shoe company. Their slogan was 'Step In - and Step Out in Style.' Further right was the narrow entrance to the Bay Horse Hotel. Dixons, where service was available 'with a smile,' (a novel idea taken up by most shops in days gone by) were having their windows cleaned by the Central Window Cleaning Co. of Leeds, the ladders for the job being transported there on a large hand cart.

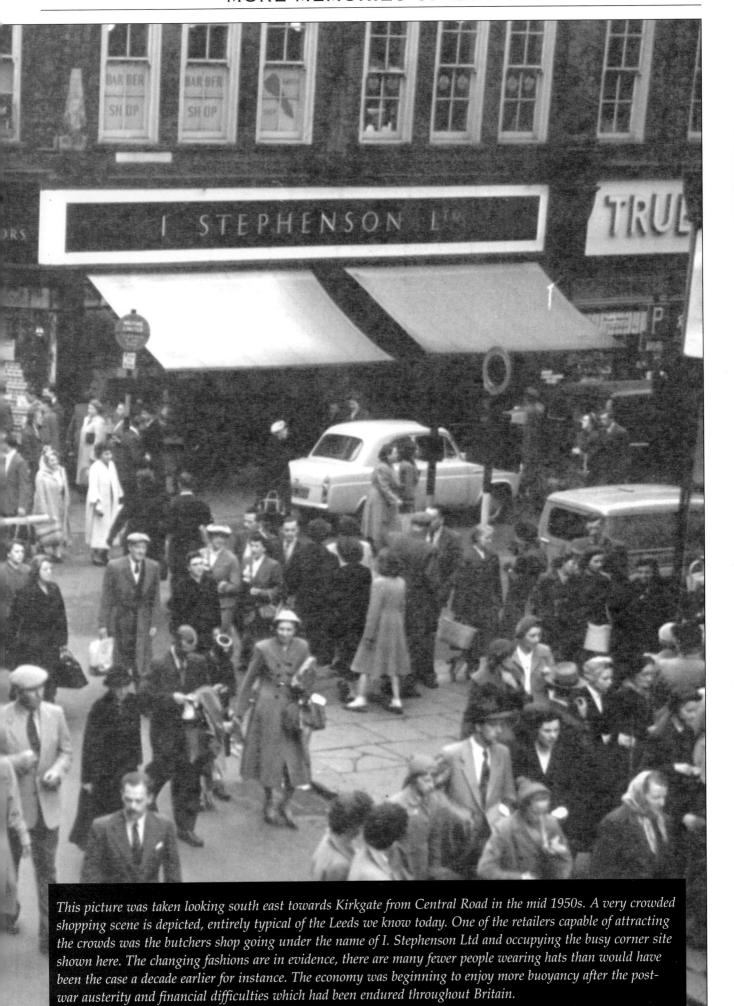

This picture was taken looking south east towards Kirkgate from Central Road in the mid 1950s. A very crowded shopping scene is depicted, entirely typical of the Leeds we know today. One of the retailers capable of attracting the crowds was the butchers shop going under the name of I. Stephenson Ltd and occupying the busy corner site shown here. The changing fashions are in evidence, there are many fewer people wearing hats than would have been the case a decade earlier for instance. The economy was beginning to enjoy more buoyancy after the post-war austerity and financial difficulties which had been endured throughout Britain.

Below: This breathtaking photograph shows the early stages of the construction of Quarry Hill Flats. It was taken in 1934. This form of construction (known as *Mopin Construction* and first perfected in France) was very advanced for its day, relying as it did on a steel framework with prefabricated concrete sections added later. The reason for this was the shortage of bricks and bricklayers for a construction project of this scale. Towns and cities throughout the country faced the problem of what to do with their slum-filled inner areas in the first half of this century. London and Liverpool were the first to replace the insanitary and overcrowded dwellings with *flats*. Manchester followed next, and one of the men responsible for the move was recruited by 'Leeds' to spearhead the replacement of the city's horrible housing around Sweet Street and replace it with a major new development. Mr R.A.H. Livett, the first Leeds City Architect and Borough Surveyor took on the challenge with gusto.

At work

This very open view of City Square dates from 1936. The old Queen's Hotel had been cleared by the demolition men in order for the version we know today to be constructed. The new hotel was opened by the Earl of Harewood in March 1937. The Black Prince looks out across to the railway station which had served the travelling public since 1846. Mill chimneys can be seen in the distance, from the 'engine room' of Leeds which created the wealth on which the city and many of its fine monuments was built. There are quite a few motor cars in the picture, though most of them are parked. The Thirties are remembered as a great motoring decade, despite the Great Depression and tremendous poverty which afflicted many families. Roads were becoming better and there was only a tiny fraction of today's number of cars in use, but amazingly the death toll on the roads in the 1930s was almost double what it is today.

Joshua Tetley & Son - 175 years of brewing in Leeds

The Joshua Tetley & Son Brewery, now part of Carlsberg Tetley Brewing, celebrated its 175th anniversary in October 1997.

William Tetley, Joshua's father was a maltster in Armley, which was then just a village near Leeds in the eighteenth century. However, the Joshua Tetley story started when the firm began brewing in the late autumn of 1822. This was the year that William Sykes' Brewery in Salem Place was bought by his friend, Joshua Tetley.

There had been a run of bad harvests, famines and the Corn Laws. Sykes could foresee only further years of loss but Joshua realised that, if he could brew the beer as well as make the malt, his position would be twice as strong. The price he paid Sykes was £409 0s 6d. Then he advertised in the Leeds Mercury, promising only to use the best ingredients. Through his knowledge and understanding of the essential ingredients required to make good beer and by buying a brewery with its own natural supply of water containing just the right mineral content, he went on to develop a range of ales that were to become legendary in Yorkshire and beyond.

To begin with, though, he failed to sell a single half pint for over a month. In the whole of the first year he sold less than £3,500 worth of beer. He was thankful at least that combining the profits from the malt and the beer put him in a stronger position.

Above left: Joshua Tetley, founder of the firm.
Below: Loading up at the brewery's bottled beer despatch department at the turn of the century. This scene was typical of the day and would have been taken before 8 o'clock in the morning.

It was more than 40 years before he could afford to stop selling malt to the gentry who used it to brew for themselves. The Earl of Derby and the Vicar of Leeds were among Joshua's regular malt customers.

Building up the brewery at Salem Place was fraught with problems and even after 26 years of work he only had 32 men working for him. Then a general rise in prosperity allowed him to double his staff and by 1886 there were over a hundred.

Within three years of Joshua's death, the younger members of the family had the confidence to tell the firm's customers that in future they would sell only beer.

By then Tetleys had such a high reputation for their ales that their customers no longer brewed for themselves.

With capital from sales, Francis Tetley, Joshua's only son, and his brother in law William Ryder were able to buy the freehold of their brewery from the Sykes-Ward family. The property by then extended to the end of Salem Place which ran over what is now Hunslet Road. Malt stores, boiler houses, chimneys and cask-washing sheds were quickly put up. Francis Tetley had had the foresight to buy land for these extensions from the owners, the Blayds-Calverley family of Oulton Hall.

Towards the turn of the century, business boomed, especially when grandson Charles came into the firm.

New offices were provided and Tetleys was selling sixty thousand barrels a year. They could have sold more if they had been able to brew it.

Above: Women maltsters, barley-driers and screens gang who served during the First World War. The picture originates from a company publication: 'A Century of Progress'.
Left: Early publicity - a showcard advertising just one of the company's products.

During all this time, Tetleys owned no pubs, although it did start providing bottled beer. This was not the success it might have been because there was no big distribution network. By 1905, however, Tetleys became a limited company, giving it access to public money.

There were light-hearted moments. In 1911 Joshua Tetley & Son challenged world famous escape artist, Harry Houdini, to escape from a padlocked metal cask filled with their ale. Houdini accepted the challenge but failed to make his escape at the Empire Theatre, Leeds. He had to be rescued by his assistant.

There were serious times too. Brewery horses remained an unbroken link with Tetleys' early times, as they do today. In November 1914, the day after war was declared, a number of Brewery horses were taken by the Royal Army Service Corps. Some were returned but many were lost. The Brewery also lost twenty five of their employees in the war out of 236 who served their country.

In the twenties came the appointment of the only member of the Tetley family to hold the position of head brewer. Edmund Herbert Tetley occupied the post for 23 years. The twenties also saw the introduction of the Brewery's famous sales emblem, the Huntsman. Created by a south west design company, the character went on to become a familiar sight to generations of beer lovers across the north, from Liverpool to Hull.

By 1950 the company owned more than 400 licensed houses and had both the money and the will to go forward.

In 1954 it linked up with the Duncan Gilmour Brewery in Sheffield which had 350 houses. Five years later, William Whitaker's in Bradford with its 119

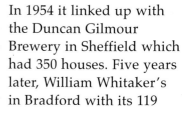

Above: Early wagon loads of Tetley's ales and stouts. **Above left:** *The Huntsman, a well-known figure to generations of drinkers.* **Left:** *Horses and drivers during the First World*

into being through the merger of Allied Breweries and Carlsberg UK. Carlsberg Tetley Brewing is now the parent company of Tetleys' Brewery and Britain's third largest brewing and wholesaling company.

Five years later, in 1996 a new £6 million Yorkshire Square fermenting vessels development was opened by international cricket umpire, Harold 'Dickie' Bird, (the man who has stood on more first class Yorkshire Squares than most people!). The new capacity made the Leeds Brewery the biggest cask ale brewery in the country

pubs also merged with Tetleys. After getting together with Melbourne Brewery in 1960 and a further partnership with Walker Cain, the Lancashire Brewery later that same year to form Tetley Walker, the company had 2771 pubs. In the mid sixties, Thomas Ramsdens of Halifax with 200 pubs and Charles Rose of Malton with 55 were to increase the size of the company further.

In 1961, Ind Coope of Burton suggested that Tetleys should come to an arrangement with them and Ansells of Birmingham on a voluntary basis. The idea was that each could preserve its individuality in day to day working, yet, when there was a need for combined research and investment they could help each other. Liking the idea, Tetleys became a member of Allied Breweries.

In 1970 came the death of the last member of the Tetley family to hold the position of chairman. He was J Noel Tetley and he ended up as President of the company. Later in the seventies Tetleys' beers won six gold medals, a silver and a bronze and the title of 'Britain's Best Pint' in the Sunday Mirror Best Beer competition.

In 1989 a new brewhouse opened to give Leeds the facility to brew Tetley's ales and, for the first time in its history, to brew lager beers.

In 1991 a new brewing distribution and sales company, Carlsberg Tetley, came

A move to merge Carlsberg Tetley and Bass Brewing was blocked by the government in June 1997 which led to Carlsberg A/S, the Copenhagen based parent of Carlsberg Lager becoming the majority shareholder of Carlsberg Tetley and so bringing together over 325 years of Danish and English brewing history.

Following this re-organisation Allied's former pubs remained within parent company, Allied Domecq, which meant that Carlsberg-Tetley became Britain's biggest *independent* brewer and wholesaler.

Above: The horses still deliver to some pubs.
Below: The Tetley Brewery now covers over 20 acres.

Brook Hansen - The electrical company that began in a stonemason's yard

Frank and Albert Parkinson were the two sons of a stonemason in Guiseley, Yorkshire. Both were engineers but Frank was an entrepreneur with a dominating personality and a brilliant commercial brain. He had the ability to inspire confidence and loyalty whilst Albert's genius lay in his mastery of precision production engineering long before those terms had any meaning for most of British industry.

When he was only 19 years old Frank had decided to go into business on his own account and, in 1908, he drew his savings of £21 out of the Post Office to found the firm F Parkinson & Co in Leeds as agents for the sale of electrical machines.

When brother Albert became associated with the venture in a shed in the stonemason's yard, a new era in the production of a.c. motors began and Parkinsons set the standard by which their competitors were judged.

They were soon on the map, patenting a constant current generator for traction, welding, search-lights, main winders and cranes. They also opened the first electrically driven tyre rolling mill.

By the end of the twenties the company was building auto-synchronous motors, the largest in the world at the time. Other work included the electrification of large industrial mining and dredging plants and large dock, sewage and water-pumping plants in this country.

The company, now F & A Parkinson Ltd, had to build larger premises at Guiseley which have since been enlarged many times.

Frank Parkinson saw in the twenties, long before anyone else, the commercial advantages of welding together complementary companies and kept his eyes open for suitable amalgamations.

An opportunity soon occurred. In 1927 he was travelling on a bus with a friend who mentioned that Cromptons were in some financial difficulty. He immediately realised that, with their d.c. machine

Above: Colonel Crompton (third left) with Frank Parkinson to his left and Albert Parkinson (second from right).
Left: Colonel Crompton, who was a legend in his own lifetime. He is pictured here with his wife.

production they could well fit into Parkinsons' plans. He was wise and generous enough to invite Colonel Crompton to join the new board even though he was long retired from active service. Frank Parkinson also gained much goodwill from his agreement to let the

Above: The Guiseley motor works with the lamp works to the left, taken in February 1938.
Below: The Guiseley Machine Shop in 1960.

Crompton name precede his own.

With a wide range of machines including large altenators and generators, switchgear,

transformers and instruments, Crompton Parkinson now moved up into the big league.

In the thirties the company formed an association with the British Electric Transformer Co Ltd and also with Derby Cables Ltd, changing the brand name of their cables from Derby to Crompton. A new lamp factory opened in Guiseley which was so successful that by 1938 Crompton lamps were being made in Australia. The company also began to manufacture house service meters.

It was a period of rapid expansion and intense activity. The initiative and enterprise in the home market was matched by overseas activity. The company's trading with India goes back to the earliest days of the electrical industry. Similar arrangements were made in Australia and production was also introduced in New Zealand and South Africa whilst the overseas sales organisation was strengthened and extended throughout the Commonwealth and many other countries. Frank Parkinson travelled the world to guide and support these ventures.

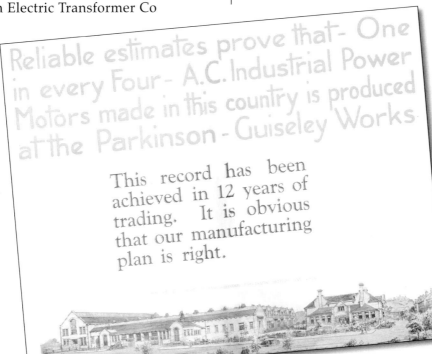

Reliable estimates prove that- One in every Four- A.C. Industrial Power Motors made in this country is produced at the Parkinson- Guiseley Works.

This record has been achieved in 12 years of trading. It is obvious that our manufacturing plan is right.

Remembering his own early days and the help which winning a scholarship had given him, in 1936 he presented Leeds University with £50,000 for the establishment of a Scholarship Endowment Fund and followed it with a gift of £200,000 for an Administration Block, which became known as the Parkinson Building.

In 1967 Crompton Parkinson became a member of the Hawker Siddeley Group. Later the electric motor interests of Crompton Parkinson were separately identified by the formation in 1973 of Crompton Parkinson Motors Ltd and these were

merged with its sister company, Brook Motors Ltd under a joint management name of Brook Crompton Parkinson Motors which changed to Brook Crompton in 1990.

In 1991 Hawker Siddeley were acquired by BTR plc. The overall product range was rationalised and the present Large Industrial Motor Division of Brook Crompton Motors Ltd was formed.

Hansen Transmissions was already a BTR company. Due to the similarity of the Hansen and Brook Crompton businesses, it was decided to integrate the two into Brook Hansen.the company currently encompasses many of the most well respected names in the design and manufacture and configuration of total drive solutions from controls through electric motors to gear units. Thus customers are provided with a consistently high standard of quality across a wide range of products around the world.

The company operates Quality Management Systems in accordance with the requirements of ISO 9001 : 1994 and holds British Standards Institute third party approval as an assessed and registered firm.

In the UK, Brook Hansen combines the strengths of Brook Crompton, Electrodrives and Bull Electric from the industrial motors field in both ac and dc machines, with those of Hansen Transmissions in the gear unit and power transmissions sectors. Brook Crompton Controls completes the picture with a full range of low voltage motor controls.

Brook Hansen is perfectly placed to provide the needs of its customers, manufacturing in Huddersfield, Honley, Blackheath,(Birmingham), Guiseley, Ipswich and Wakefield. So, the establishment by the Parkinson brothers of a solidly based, progressive and competitive electrical manufacturing industry has led to Brook Hansen, world leader in its field.

Above: The motor despatch department at Guiseley in October 1948. *Facing page, top:* An early leaflet promoting the company's product. *Facing page, bottom:* The Guiseley winding shop in 1959.

A success storey!

Although being 100 years old this year, family owned packaging printer Storey Evans cannot possibly be accused of being set in its ways. The company is proud of the true Yorkshire grit image and holds fast to the qualities embodied in Larkfield Mill, a splendid industrial building, which has been the company's home since before the First World War.

A truly family business George Frederick Storey who founded the business was the present managing director's grandfather. He was born in 1873 and apprenticed with McCorquodale & Co Ltd, a local printing firm.

The early days
Striking out on his own he set up a small printing business in Park Square, Leeds, in 1898, providing a general printing

service. By 1911 the business had grown to such an extent that a move was made to Larkfield Mill, Rawdon, where the company converted part of the mill to a Printing Works. Storey Evans still occupies these premises today.

Larkfield Mill was built in 1824 as a woollen mill, one of the first in the country to process Australian wool. It had the Victorian virtue of combining robustness and elegance and even now its outward appearance is not much changed.

Records show that in December 1922 Storey Evans petitioned the great H. G. Wells to use a quotation from one of his books 'The Salvaging of Civilisation'. At the time the company was producing advertising for local opticians and the author gave his permission (*see above right*).

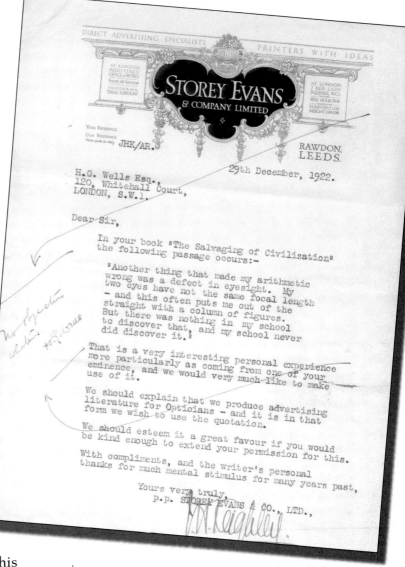

Before 1939 Storey Evans began producing cardboard cartons. The two world wars had brought a shortage of materials but after the second war Mr H F Storey was able to bring litho-printing techniques to Storey Evans.

It was not until the 1950s that the decision was taken to concentrate on the carton market but the company is now acknowledged to be amongst the most professional of carton makers with a wide customer base of industries including pharmaceuticals, healthcare, food and DIY.

Expansion

Having become a significant force in the carton industry, Storey Evans, in the early 1970s decided to diversify into roll-feed labels because their existing customers expressed a need for a label supplier to match their level of dependability and quality in cartons. They produce a great variety of pharmaceutical, toiletry, bakery, food and hardware labels.

Much of their output runs on automatic lines and there are facilities for isolating maximum security jobs. Later, Visual Carded Packaging became a significant part of the Storey Evans product mix.

Above: The letter to H. G. Wells, dating from December 1922, duly signed and returned by the author.
Left: A charming turn of the century picture.
Facing page top: Larkfield Mill circa 1840.

They became associated with MY Sharp Interpack who were acknowledged leaders in plastic forming and so were able to offer a guaranteed system of cards, blisters and sealing machinery.

Expansion into the European market was achieved by the acquisition of the company's Dutch subsidiary, Spruyt Holland, in 1990.

During that year the company was commissioned to produce four million commemorative coin holders for the Queen Mother's 90th birthday.

Another initiative of the early nineties was a £750,000 investment in additional self adhesive labels production which

in 1991 accounted for 20% of the firm's business.

The company is deliberately self-sufficient in its facilities and operations. Their policy of continuous plant renewal has resulted in an impressive range of up-to-date printing and carton making machinery. The factory environment is clean, bright and well cared for.

Accreditation to BS 5750 Part 2 (ISO 9002) was achieved in 1989. Then, in 1992 the company became accredited to the Pharmaceutical Supplier Code of Practice. Recently it has recieved accreditation to Investors in People.

A large number of internationally-known customers have been with the company for many years.

Storey Evans attribute their success partly to their ability to supply a wide range of quantities. No order is too large, but, at the same time, they are flexible and offer their customers small runs. All orders get a quick response.

Future plans include moving to a new 11.8 acre site in 1998. The company will be sorry to leave the old mill building but pleased to expand their business yet again.

Above: Goods inwards entrance in the original mill building. *Facing page, top:* M.P. Sir Giles Shaw commissions Storey Evans' multi-colour printing press in 1979. *Facing page, bottom:* The late Chairman, Hadrian Storey, wife Eileen and Sir Giles Shaw at the ceremony. *Below:* Office staff in the early 1970s.

James Hare Ltd - from a lowly cottage to nationwide service

The manufacture of cloth has for centuries been an important occupation of Yorkshire men and women. There is proof of the existence of the industry from the 12th century onwards and generations of the people of Leeds have worked at the spinning wheel, the loom and the dye vat.

It has been claimed that the history of James Hare Ltd is the history of Leeds, since its growth followed proportionately the industrial growth of the city itself.

James Hare, the founder, began work in the middle of the 19th century as an apprentice in a worsted mill. Within a short time, he had displayed such a quick grasp of commercial practice that he was accepted as one of the best judges of quality and value in wool and worsted cloth.

Able and energetic, Hare was a Yorkshireman and therefore also cautious. He began his independent career by purchasing from his employers piece ends and remnants which he sold to railway workers going from Leeds to London. They, in turn, sold them to relatives and friends in the south. Hare always gave full value for money rather than seeking a large profit on any single transactions. So, this business, which began in a cottage in the 1860s, grew so rapidly that Mr Hare was soon able to set himself up as a woollen and worsted merchant.

At first he sold to all comers from his cottage-shop but soon he had enough business from catering solely for the tailoring trade. In due course he took a small warehouse in Wellington Street and was joined in the business by his brother Samuel and his cousin Robert Sykes.

He realised from the start that the chief factor of success was good relations. An artist-craftsman with high ideals, he constantly set himself higher standards of quality. His sons, Arthur and Clifford, who

Above left: James Hare.
Left: First premises in Clare Street.
Right: Dixon & Gaunt Ltd machine room.

succeeded him adhered to the principles he had taught them.

In 1913 it was decided to launch into the actual manufacture of cloth. The firm bought a comparatively small shed to accommodate seven looms and there the famous K serges were first made. From this small beginning Arlington Mills developed to cover several acres with sixteen bays of weaving sheds and modern-for-the-time looms weaving fine quality plain and semi plain worsteds known as K quality productions and Ritzie worsted flannels.

In 1922 a large reserve warehouse was purchased in Queen Street. Later, adjoining property was demolished and Coronet House erected, more than doubling the capacity of the original structure. The work was completed just before the second world war and for some time these two buildings formed the headquarters of the organisation. James Hare was the first company in the north of England to install a teleprinter link with their London offices. In 1922 when this revolutionary step was taken the city of Leeds was startled to realise the speed with which orders from London could be handled. For many years every tailor was familiar with James Hare's famous Coronet bunches. They were supplied free to tailors "of standing" and consisted of graded samples of the cloths produced by "every manufacturer.

The company was proud that its K cloths were always free from weavers' faults. Their looms, of the newest available type were installed so that the power and tension was always uniform. Every weaver had to pass stringent tests before being placed in charge of a loom. The huge production enabled the weavers to continue the same numbers on the same looms without interference. Always working the same class of yarn under the same conditions, they had a great advantage over manufacturers who were constantly requiring to change.

During the first war, when the dye trade was in chaos, Hares were the only people who unconditionally guaranteed their dyewares. The most important process was finishing and so the shrinking and preparation to make the cloth right for the tailors' irons were carefully supervised. When the pieces reached the warehouse they were minutely examined before being despatched to the tailor.

In 1933 the company acquired Dixon & Gaunt Ltd to provide a first class Cut, Make and Trim service for James Hare Ltd's vast clientele.

In 1952 the group established a subsidiary company in Canada.

Above: Preparing bunches for despatch to the tailors.
Left: An early exhibition stand.

James Hare (Canada) Ltd carried stock in Montreal, issued bunches to tailors throughout Canada and carried on business in similar style to its parent company in England. Five years later another subsidiary was established in Hamburg, Germany.

For many decades the company was well known throughout the world for high quality suiting and tweeds and in 1973 the international trading style of 'Hare of England' was sold with the mens merchanting business to the Illingworth Morris Group of Bradford.

Since that time the fourth generation of the family have set about the task of regenerating all the warehousing properties in Wellington Street and Queen Street as well as developing a multi-tenanted industrial complex on the site of their old mill in Armley.

However, more than this they have perpetuated the Hare name in the world of textiles by creating one of the largest distributors of silk fabrics in Europe - James Hare Silks.

The James Hare Group has truly changed with the times - rather like the City of Leeds and its people.

Above: The packing and despatch department.
Left: The London office showroom.
Below: The warehouses in Queen Street.

Sixty years of progress for the north's leading property company

The new headquarters of Evans of Leeds was opened by the Lord Mayor of Leeds, Councillor J L Carter, in April 1990. This flagship building at Millshaw on the Leeds Ring Road celebrated fifty years of progress and growth for one of the north's leading property companies.

Now the building is eight years old and it is almost sixty years since Fred Evans created the company that was, in his lifetime, to control property throughout the country and claim as its tenants some of the top companies in British industry and commerce. Its investment companies currently hold assets of more than £300 million and shareholders' funds exceed £181 million.

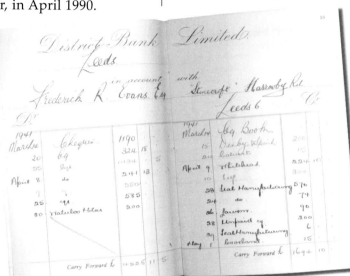

Frederick Redvers Evans, to give him his full title, was proudly named after General Redvers Buller who led his men in the Boer War. Fred Evans was an Army boxing champion during his own military service. In peacetime, he bought his own delivery vehicle from the widow

of a former friend and in addition to carrying out house furniture removals, transported furniture from its manufacturers in London to retailers in Leeds.

The business began in Waterloo Street in a single-storey building which is now part of the Tetley complex. Later, a move was made to Waterloo Mills, Waterloo Lane, Bramley.

The Waterloo theme was continued with the Telex/Telegraphic address which was 'Waterloo Leeds'.

The roots of the Evans group go back to pre-war south Leeds when Mr Fred Evans began to build a thriving plant hire business. During the War the company was involved in plant hire and civil engineering. Much of the plant was used in the construction of airfields and open cast coal mining.

After the war, he began to add some astutely purchased sites, mainly redundant war-time airfields, to form the basis of the present property portfolio.

Above: A letterhead dating from 1964.
Top: 1964 picture of Millshaw headquarters.
Facing page, top: A bank book from the Second World War.
Facing page, bottom: Former laundry premises at Austhorpe, Leeds, purchased by Evans in 1964, sold some time later.

Some house building was done in the forties and fifties with a partner named Eric Scott and together they built the Southleigh Estate off Dewsbury Road.

By 1962, Mr Evans knew the company needed larger headquarters if it was to make further progress. He obtained temporary planning permission and built his new headquarters on a former open cast coal site at Millshaw on the outskirts of Leeds which he had bought from Farnley Estates. Permanent planning permission was granted many years later. It was another example of his foresight. The open countryside that surrounded his spot became one of the major commercial areas of the city's suburbs where premises are keenly sought by major companies.

The first headquarters building was a functional two-storey design typical of the early sixties. By 1969 however Evans had outgrown it, so a second building was constructed,

silver jubilee celebrations in 1996. He played a most important part in steering the company in a relentless drive for rent roll growth. Mr Curtis remains a non-executive member of the Board, offering his wisdom and experience.

The management team is presently headed by John Bell who joined the company in 1994 from Yorkshire Water. The policies so strongly advocated by George Best are still followed and rental income now stands in excess of £29 million a year. The company has a cautious and modest development programme in which the majority of its properties are pre-let. This contributes to the capital growth.

connected to the first by a bridge and in an architectural style less likely to become dated.

In 1971, under the personal guidance and direction of Michael Evans, the family floated the company. They employed the services of Hambros Bank and solicitors Travers Smith Braithwaite. Cecil Berens, a director of Hambros, became the company's first chairman and the connection with Hambros has continued to the present time.

After the flotation of the company Mr Evans continued to invest in industrial property. Recently, however, it was decided to alter the balance of the portfolio and include commercial and retail investments. Soon, even the enlarged Millshaw headquarters were hard pressed to cope with the increasing size of the group. So, the decision was taken to rebuild the headquarters yet again. This time the style is classical and the building adds dignity to an area of Leeds already graced by the premises of major banks and other prestigious organisations.

For much of the period since flotation, the company was in the extremely competent hands of Ernest Curtis and George Best. Mr Best died in 1994 and was sadly missed at the company's

The Group continues to expand, currently employing a staff of sixty five under the direction of the main board which is chaired by John Padovan. Michael Evans is Vice-Chairman and his three sons, Roderick, Andreas and Dominic are members of the Board.

"THE COMPANY HAS A CAUTIOUS AND MODEST DEVELOPMENT PROGRAMME"

Fred Evans died in 1992, leaving the company in the capable hands of his family who still remain the principal shareholders, providing stability and continuity and enabling the company to make long term plans unaffected by short term factors.

For the future, the company will continue to follow the business strategy which has served it so well in the past. The quality of its rent roll, the strength of its balance sheet, the development potential of its existing sites, the prospects for its joint venture companies and the assured success of the White Rose Shopping Centre should enable it to maintain steady progress in the years ahead.

Above: Evans' premises at Millshaw.
Facing page, top: A 1969 aerial view of the site at Millshaw.
Facing page, bottom: The impressive interior of the Millshaw premises.

Oilgear Towler - a step back into history

The hydraulic engineering company Oilgear Towler is one of the largest businesses in the small village of Rodley, and also one of the oldest. The history of the company contains many developments which will be of interest to engineers and non-engineers alike.

On February 26th 1913 Mr. John Robert Pickering and Mr. James Arthur Towler purchased an engineering company from William Deighton and Harold Loxton. The first legal documents relating to the company under its new owners go back to March 17th 1913 when it was incorporated as the Leeds Engineering and Hydraulic Company Limited.

Surviving letterheads indicate that a company of the same name had been established in 1886 and had gone into liquidation a short time previously. Wishing to capitalise on the reputation and goodwill, the Towlers and Mr. Pickering retained the name.

Above right: Frank Towler in 1952.
Below: The company's certificate of incorporation from 1913.

In May of that year a meeting was held which was attended by six senior members of the company. Mr. John Robert Pickering was appointed chairman, and the minute book suggests that he and Mr. James Alfred Towler were the meeting's most active participants.

Messrs Pickering and Clapham leaving the company, which consequently changed its name to Towler Brothers (Patents) Limited. Now the Towler brothers had become the controlling force. In 1933 Frank Towler formed his own company, Electraulic Presses Limited, which allowed him to exercise his patent rights and designs without any interference from the board of the family company.

The brothers produced pumps, valves and systems through to the mid fifties. The range included the In-line pumps, the Z axial pumps and the Autodraulic control systems for forging presses. Throughout these years the Board Meeting minutes show that there were considerable efforts made to overcome technical problems. This resulted in technological advancements which brought the company to the forefront of the hydraulics industry. In 1952 the company supplied the first direct oil

The premises were in Rodley where the company remains to this day.

The Directors' report of 1918 tells us that, after five years in office, Mr. Pickering died. His son succeeded him on the Board of Directors and Mr. James Alfred Towler was elected to be the next chairman. His two sons, John Maurice and Frank Hathorn Towler came into the company, the former being elected a Director in 1927.

After his father's death John Maurice Towler became the dominant Director. He was joined on the Board by his brother Frank in 1931.

In the years between 1931 and 1935 there appear to have been board room difficulties between the Towler brothers and the rest, notably Messrs Pickering and Clapham. This dispute resulted in

Right: John Towler in August 1952.
Above: Edward Orchard worked as a commissioning engineer for nearly forty years. He was awarded the MBE for his service to exports. He is pictured here with his wife outside Buckingham Palace.

hydraulic drive on a forging press to Soderfors in Sweden. November 1954 brought the opening of a Towler German office in Dusseldorf.

In 1958, after the death of John Towler, Metal Industries Limited bought the whole of Towler Brothers (Patents) Limited and their holdings in Electraulic Presses Limited and Redam. Redam were a French company in which some of the directors of

Towler Brothers and Electraulic Presses held shares. They represented Towler in France and Belgium. The Towler family connection remained with Frank Towler, now chairman, and his son James who was also employed within the company.

In the late fifties the electronic thickness control for forging presses was developed. Minutes of a meeting in December 1958 record thanks to a

Mr. Tom White for his work on patenting this process. Throughout the fifties there had been discussions about designing and manufacturing vane pumps and entering the medium pressure valve market.

Available government grants allowed a factory to be built at Maydown in Northern Ireland. Vane pumps were made in Northern Ireland in the sixties and Repetition Hydraulics was formed to market Towler vane pumps from Maydown. This was a difficult market to penetrate at that time and the company eventually stopped making vane pumps when the Northern Ireland factory closed.

The industrial valve business was much more successful. This product range was made in Eaglescliffe in the North of England, and by Schwelm & Towler in Germany. Their production was the forerunner of the current European Parker industrial valve range. To compete in the market, Towlers identified the need to design competitive pumps with servo-controls.

In 1967 Mr. Frank Hathorn Towler resigned, dissatisfied with the acquisition of Metal Industries Limited by Thorn Electrical Industries and the lack of investment. The loss of Mr Towler's services broke the Towler family ties with the company. At this point it changed its name to Towler Hydraulics Limited and made a licensing agreement with Kelsey Hayes Company in the USA.

The seventies began with the building of a new office block, the contract for it being signed in June 1971. Two years later Towler Pilgrim Limited was formed from the old MI Group Regional Offices Limited with the purpose of developing a 3000 horsepower transmission pump to be used on P&O oil transfer barges. This project was an interesting exercise and resulted in the building of a new development test bed. However, support was withdrawn following the building of suitable berthing for large tankers at oil terminals.

Throughout the seventies the company worked closely with ASEA in Sweden on deep drawing presses, fluid cell presses and isostatic presses working at pressures of up to 100,000 psi. This work required both hydraulic and electronic expertise. By the late seventies the company had become involved with microprocessor technology and commissioned its first micro-processor controlled system in 1978.

The mid seventies were a time of great change. In 1974 Towler Hydraulics Limited purchased the assets of Pressure Dynamics Limited and obtained the FCS pump which Pressure

Below: An aerial view of the company's premises dating from the 1960s.

> "THE COMPANY COMMISSIONED ITS FIRST MICROPROCESSOR CONTROLLED SYSTEM IN 1978"

Dynamics had designed as a development of the Towler series D pump. A lease was signed for the Grangefield factory in Pudsey. In the following year Towler acquired Bradford Cylinders Limited and the Eaglescliffe factory was sold to Cargo Fleet Chemical Company Limited. In 1978 the agreement with Kelsey Hayes was terminated and Towler Hydraulics set up their own factory in Ubana, Ohio. In December 1979 dealings became even more complicated. Pratt Precision changed its name to Towler Hydraulics (UK) Limited which then acquired Towler Hydraulics Limited. Pratt Precision and Towler Hydraulics Limited became dormant. This resulted in the Pratt Precision Hydraulics company number being passed on to Oilgear Towler Limited when that company came into being.

This happened in July 1985 when the Oilgear Company of Milwaukee acquired Towler Hydraulics (UK) Limited from Thorn EMI.

Oilgear saw the opportunity to use the Leeds company as its European manufacturing centre and about 35% of Oilgear Towler's output goes directly for export. Typical markets for the company's hydraulic systems are the steel industry, wood and rubber manufacturers, civil engineering and defence applications.

Following the acquisition, The Oilgear Company embarked on a substantial investment programme which included computer aided design, further development of the electronics arm of the business and sophisticated machine tools.

As the new millennium approaches, Oilgear Towler are growing from strength to strength. What began as a small family business has now flourished into an established and highly respected world-wide organisation.

Despite its international connections, Oilgear Towler is a company that has remained close to its roots. The main UK site is still based in Rodley, unobtrusively hidden away from the surrounding rural community.

Oilgear Towler's loyalty to the region is clear in their choice of business associates; the vast majority of companies they choose to deal with are Leeds based, whether they be suppliers, printers or manufacturers. Local charities have benefited from fund-raising ventures, and a medal-winning athletics team is also active. In contrast, Oilgear Towler's customers are spread far and wide across the globe.

Although steeped in history, Oilgear Towler are constantly looking to the future. The research facilities at the Leeds site are second to none; new products are constantly being developed, and existing products are adapted to reach new speeds and pressures. State of the art three dimensional computer design systems are used to visualize new concepts and ideas before on-site construction. New ways to solve problems hydraulically are developed on a daily basis.

The Towler company has come a long way since its formation all those years ago. Together with The Oilgear Company, Oilgear Towler look set to take electro-hydraulic engineering to unprecedented heights in the new millennium.

Above: A drawing press dating from the 1950s.
Left: A visit by the Navy with Frank Towler (son of the founder) on the left.

Pennine Castings - putting the spark of life into millions of shoes

Many of us still remember the Blakey's Segs, Hob Nails and Tacketty Boots. During the Great War, the Army marched on thousands of tons of Blakey's studs. Even today, the armies of several countries still march on boot protectors made by Pennine Castings (formerly Blakey's).

Though people chiefly remember the clunking noises they could make walking along the street, the real purpose of the studs was to prolong the life of their shoes.

In 1880, Mr John Blakey, a prolific inventor, accidentally got a piece of metal in his boot sole whilst walking. He then found that, whilst the rest of the tread wore away, the part where the metal remained was unworn. This gave him the idea for a protective metal piece to be hammered into the sole.

The present company was founded in 1902 and took over several others who manufactured similar products. It built up export markets until at one time it was supplying 40 countries and currently almost 20% of their turnover goes overseas.

Above: An early advertisement for Heel Tips.
Right: Part of the production process.

The company grew by acquisition and also expanded its product range into general castings, fasteners, chains and conduit fittings.

In 1978, the Company was taken over by a PLC but then in 1988, a management buy-out brought it back into private ownership. Unfortunately the recession followed shortly after, forcing the management to retrench the business and operate on a much smaller scale, going back to its traditional product lines.

Eight years on, the company currently employ 25 people and turnover is in excess of £1 million. Many of the products that went out to other

partner out and is now the sole owner and director.

Pennine's range covers a broad sphere of products for such industries as small tools, building and construction, DIY, water, gas, electrical, railways, engineering, hardware, ironmongery and mining. Its customer base includes such household names as Rawlplug, Woolworths, Timpson, Reckitt & Colman, Stanley, and Draper and larger concerns such as the National Coal Board, The Ministry of Defence and Balfour Beatty.

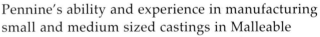

foundries have been recovered and they have expanded into producing the electrical installation and support castings as well as forever increasing their range of DIY products which now represents almost 50% of the turnover and includes such items as Hammer Wedges which hold the metal hammer head onto the wooden shaft, Door Bolts, Gate Strikers, Door Handles, Window Closers and Latches, Pipe Saddles and Clamps, to name but a few. In June 1997, Peter Black bought his

Pennine Castings have invested quite heavily in new and modern equipment with the assistance of a Diversification and Technology grant from the Leeds Development Agency, assisted by Business Link and a further grant is allowing them to have new promotional literature printed. This has allowed them to increase capacity and efficiency by better utilisation of their resources.

Pennine's ability and experience in manufacturing small and medium sized castings in Malleable and Grey Irons, means that they have retained a niche in a very competitive market. They believe their success is due to them offering a reliable service, goods of the best quality, a short delivery and a superior finish. The firm is as happy to fulfill small orders as large ones.

This year marks the 96th anniversary of the company which still survives and intends through the investments recently made, to prosper in the new century.

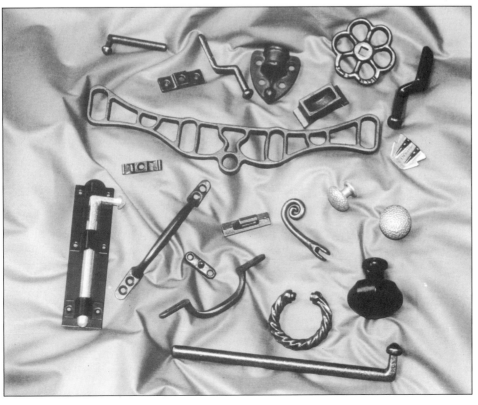

Top: Two adverts aimed at the overseas market. Left: Some of the company's products today.

Braime Pressings - over 100 years of pedigree

Whilst quite a few well-known engineering firms have vanished from the Hunslet scene, the family firm of T F & J H Braime has stood the test of time.

The family has its roots in the village of Rothwell. In the middle of the last century Mr George Braime was the local veterinary surgeon. He and his wife Mary had three children.

Thomas, the eldest was apprenticed to the Hunslet engineers McLaren, which meant for him an early walk to work and a late walk home at night.

Later, an accident in which he lost his thumb gave Thomas the chance to work on an idea which had been germinating in his mind for some time. In 1888, he therefore took a small building

Above: A photograph taken in 1953 to commemorate 50 years in service. From left to right: D. Hodgson, J.E. Ward, J. Saville and T.F. Braime. Below: A general view of the press shop in the early 1920s.

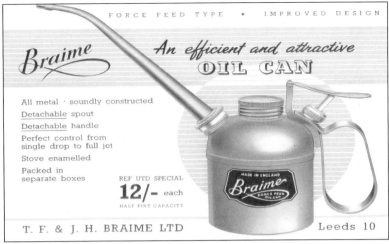

FORCE FEED TYPE • IMPROVED DESIGN

Braime

An efficient and attractive
OIL CAN

All metal · soundly constructed
Detachable spout
Detachable handle
Perfect control from
single drop to full jet
Stove enamelled
Packed in
separate boxes

REF UTD SPECIAL
12/- each
HALF PINT CAPACITY

T. F. & J. H. BRAIME LTD   Leeds 10

in Leake Street, Hunslet and began producing small pressings with a flypress and fabricating oilcans.

A little while later the Rothwell Times reported that, 'The well known patent steel oil can brought out by (Braime) is becoming extensively used.' Orders had come in from Adelaide and Melbourne. Rio de Janeiro, Newfoundland and Christiania.

The demand for his small pressings encouraged Thomas to look for larger premises where he could expand his business. He moved, first into Glasshouse Street and later into Donisthorpe Street, off Goodman Street, Hunslet. Such progress was made with the metal pressings that Thomas was joined in his business by his brother Harry.

Harry was a man of abounding energy. Although trained to follow his father as a veterinary surgeon, he had a great engineering brain and, with his help, the firm grew and progressed further.

The rise of the motoring industry increased the demand for metal pressings and soon even larger premises were needed. Plans were put under way for a new factory to be built on vacant land bounded by Sayner Lane, Carlisle Street and Brookfield Street.

The new factory opened in 1911 and was fully operational in time to take an active part in the war effort between 1914 and 1918. In 1917 a the brothers built the first works canteen in Leeds in order to provide hot meals for its new female workers. The canteen was opened by Princess Mary. Between the two wars the excellence of its dance floor was renowned.

In 1930 Mr Harry Braime died and was interred in the grave of his father and mother in Rothwell churchyard. Mr Thomas Braime lived to be 94 and was active in the firm throughout the second war. At no time did the brothers forget the village where they had been born. The partners always took a fatherly interest in their employees. In the fifties, in recognition of their loyalty, Braimes were pioneers in the creation of a profit sharing scheme.

The firm is still going strong under the directorship of the grandsons of Harry Braime. It is situated on a four acre site and employs 150 people. It is a major supplier to a wide range of industries including the automotive, commercial vehicle, fire prevention, commercial catering, material handling, medical, petrochemical, refrigeration and utility industries and of components for Conveyors and Elevators sold world-wide. The company won the Queen's Award for Export in 1998.

Above: A brochure dating from 1952. **Left:** *Modern equipment means that the company can maintain the highest standards.*

A household name for quality wallpaper

Firth, Ray & Prosser date back to 1871 when James Henry Prosser and Andrew Ray set up in Birmingham as Ray & Prosser, both having worked for Potters of Darwen (now Crown Wallcoverings).

Leeds with its excellent rail system was chosen for a foray into Yorkshire. Charles Firth was taken on as a partner to run the Leeds business which began in Lower Albion Street, below the old Co-op building. Larger premises were soon taken further up Albion Street. Andrew Ray died without issue in 1890.

At the turn of the century most of the UK wallpaper mills merged or were taken over to form the Wallpaper Manufacturers Ltd. Fearing the power of this group, the merchants formed the Wallpaper Merchants' Association. The success of this meant that for the next 60 or so years the trade was regulated by these two groups. James Henry Prosser was founding president of the latter but he died, aged 59 from food poisoning at a hotel, leaving Charles Firth as senior partner. He too died early leaving no successors.

Ray & Prosser.
WHOLESALE
PAPER HANGINGS WAREHOUSE,
22, Smallbrook Street,
BIRMINGHAM.

By then the Prosser sons, Henry, Allan and Edward had entered the business. Henry, the oldest, moved to Yorkshire and took over the running of FRP. His first job was to find new premises as the business had again outgrown its current ones. He bought a wool warehouse in Wellington Street. After extensive alteration the site became the firm's home in 1903.

Henry Prosser died aged 47. (This was obviously not a healthy industry). Allan and Edward then ran the two businesses from Birmingham and both lived to retire.

By the twenties another generation had joined the business in the persons of James Henry and Allan Leslie, sons of Henry, and Geoffrey, son of Edward. Allan Leslie served with distinction in the first war, being wounded twice and awarded the MC. He and James Henry came up to Leeds and were made partners in the thirties. Geoffrey died in 1960 and his son Alan took over in Birmingham until that part of the business was sold to A Sanderson Ltd in 1970. James Henry's sons, David and John, are now joint managing directors.

Many Leeds people will remember the disastrous fire that gutted the Wellington Street warehouse in 1963. Fortunately no-one was hurt and the business

survived. After the fire premises were rented in Harehills Lane. When a new site was found a warehouse and offices were built and the company moved to its present address in January 1971.

Meanwhile, beginning in 1889, John Gray worked for the firm, establishing and running the paint department. He was responsible for the appointment by the Walpamur company (now Crown Paints) of FRP as the sole distributor for their products in the West Riding. This was the foundation of FRP's future success with paints. John Gray died in 1952, having risen to general manager. After war service and his father's death, his son Allan took over the management of the paint department. He became managing director in 1970 and continued as chairman after he retired in 1990 until he died in 1993.

There have been many changes in the business since the early days. Wallpaper distribution up to the sixties was usually by rail. Since then it has been by express overnight service via roads. There have been big changes in retail trade with the growth of super-

stores. The company, from being a regional wallpaper wholesaler, has become a locally focused decorators' merchant.

Today FRP offers a vast range of products for professional decorators and contractors. Firth, Ray and Prosser are proud of the fact that, although it is a small local company, its wallcoverings are regularly used for commercial work throughout the UK and recent orders have been sent as far afield as Moscow and Hong Kong.

It is looking forward to the challenges of the new millennium and entering its third century of trading with confidence and enthusiasm.

Above: The disastrous fire in 1963 gutted the Wellington Street premises. Fortunately no-one was hurt and the business survived.
Facing page, top: James Henry Prosser and his wife, Mary-Ann with their sons in the late 1800s.
Facing page, centre left: An early Business card.
Facing page, bottom: The Wellington Street premises in the late 1950s.

Abraham Moon - from humble beginnings to international renown

Eighteen thirty seven is a memorable year in at least two respects. It was the year in which Queen Victoria succeeded to the British throne. It was also the year in which Abraham Moon founded the company which today holds an enviable status as one of the country's leading woollen and worsted manufacturers.

Abraham Moon, a figure of considerable standing in the community of Guiseley, on the northern fringes of Leeds and the southern fringes of the Yorkshire Dales, supplied many local families with yarn to weave cloth on hand looms in their homes. When the

cloth was woven he would collect the pieces, paying the weavers for their work. The cloth was then scoured (washed) locally and hung out to dry in the surrounding fields. Abraham would then transport the pieces by horse and cart to Leeds for sale in the market.

In 1868 Moon had a three storey mill built on Netherfield Road in Guiseley, less than three hundred yards from his house at the top of Oxford Avenue. The mill had an abundant source of local water which was soft and ideal for scouring and other processes necessary in woollen manufacture. The newly built railway to Leeds ran directly behind the mill which had its own sidings.

Above: The finishing department, 1937.
Left: Building work on the original mill, 1868.
Facing page, top: Directors and office staff 1913. Charles Walsh (third from right, seated), Frank Walsh (far right, seated). Facing page, bottom: Part of Moon's transport fleet! Circa 1910. The little girl is thought to be Hilda Hollins.

This proved an invaluable form of transport both inward (wool for processing, coal for power) and outward (distribution of cloth to the expanding customer network). The company's records show exports to countries including Japan as early as the 1890s.

In August 1877 Abraham Moon lost his life in an accident. A report from a local newspaper of the time sets the scene: "Mr Moon was attending the annual Yeadon feast in his horse-

drawn carriage. When a band struck up the startled horse bolted down Henshaw Lane. Two passengers managed to jump clear and were unharmed but Mr Moon stayed in his carriage trying to calm the horse. In its panic it tried to turn into a familiar lane where there was no room for the carriage. The vehicle demolished part of a wall into which Abraham Moon was thrown. He died soon afterwards from a head injury". The article goes on to report that the horse survived the accident!

Abraham's son Isaac succeeded him in the business which continued to flourish, but in 1902 the original multi-storey mill burned to the ground. Undeterred Isaac Moon built a much larger single storey mill. There was a large pool of skilled textile workers in Guiseley and none of Moon's workforce had far to walk as the new

mill occupied a central position in Guiseley. By this time the mill had become fully 'vertical' i.e. all processes - dyeing, blending, carding, spinning, weaving and finishing taking place on one site.

Design and pattern books which date back to the early part of the Twentieth Century tell a story in themselves. Fashion fabrics from 1900 to 1913 gradually give way to army shirting, trouserings and greatcoat cloths from 1914 which in turn are replaced by the emerging fashion of the 20s. Today designers still use the old pattern books for inspiration and the creation of retro looks.

Isaac Moon took the business forward until his death in 1909. In its obituary column the local newspaper reports that Isaac was taken ill on 2nd July, shortly after watching England play - presumably versus Australia - in a test match at Headingley (it doesn't report whether this was the cause of the illness!)

In 1920 the Moon family sold their shares in the company in order to pursue other interests. The shares were purchased by Charles H Walsh who was both designer and mill manager at the time. Charles borrowed the sum of £33,000 to buy the

*Above: The boiler house pictured in the Centenary year, 1937. **Top left:** The Dye House, 1937. **Far left:** The sorting and blending department in 1912.*

business and it took him the rest of his lifetime to repay it.

Charles Walsh died in 1924 and the company then passed to his son Frank who was already in the business. Thirty years later Frank's nephew Arthur took control and remains chairman to this day. The current managing director is John Walsh, the fourth generation of the family which succeeded the Moon dynasty.

The company continues to grow from strength to strength despite the massive contraction of the woollen industry since

Export Achievement. This in addition to numerous design awards received in recent years.

Company policy has always emphasised the need to re-invest profits in capital machinery resulting in modern plant, production control systems and computer aided design and manufacturing technology. As a vertical company 'Moon' are in an ideal position to give their customers an

1950. Then there were seven woollen manufacturers in Guiseley, now there is one.

Renowned for traditional values of quality, the company has in recent years developed an enviable worldwide reputation for design and colour flair. Exports currently account for some 70% of turnover - U.S.A., Germany, Italy, France and Japan being the major markets. In 1996 Moon won the prestigious Queen's Award for

unparalleled service - vital in these times of 'fast response' and 'just-in-time' manufacturing. They look to the future with high expectations.

Above: The works canteen pictured in the Centenary year, 1937. *Below:* The first Mill trip (to the Winter Gardens in Blackpool, 1946).
Facing page top: The Warping Department in 1937.
Facing page bottom: The Burling and Mending department, 1937.

Keeping Britain's industry on the road

The Pelican Engineering Company was originally formed in 1919 by Mr Ernest Crump when the army no longer required his services as a dispatch rider at the end of the First World War. At the time of his discharge his entire worldly possessions could be carried in one suitcase but undeterred, he decided to employ skills he had learned from the army in civilian life. Searching for an original name, he remembered his regimental mascot, the Pelican, and transferred the name to his new business hoping it would bring him good fortune there too.

He used his army discharge pay to place a deposit on a small shed at Scout Hill, Dewsbury and within 12 months he was employing four men busily engaged in converting surplus military vehicles into a road worthy specification. By 1928, the company was doing so much business that it needed to move to larger premises in Pepper Road, Hunslet, Leeds. The principal reason for the rapid success was the

company's close association with Gardner Engines of Patricroft Manchester, who at the time, were the largest manufacturer of diesel oil engines in the country. In 1931 Pelican was made an official agent for Gardner oil engines confirming a partnership that would last for over 50 years.

Between 1931 and 1940 the company carried out over 800 conversions,

removing petrol engines from buses and trucks and replacing them with Gardner diesel engines. Also during the thirties, Pelican became involved with Foden Trucks of Sandbach, Cheshire whose vehicles were becoming an increasingly common sight on the roads. Like Pelican, Foden at the time was a family run business with a history dating back to the steam engines of the previous century. In 1934 Pelican became the official Yorkshire selling agent for Foden Trucks.

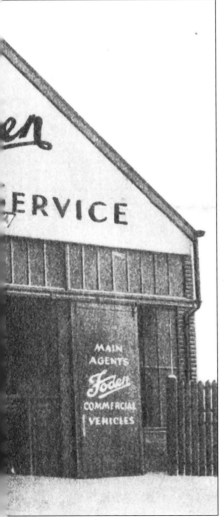

Throughout the Second World War, Pelican worked almost exclusively for the Ministry of Defence, involved in the preparation and refurbishment of army trucks which meant the firm was able to grow further during these most difficult of times. By 1946 the business had out grown the Pepper Road site and the decision was again taken to move. A suitable building was not easy to find and Mr Crump settled on the old tram workshops at Bell Hill, Rothwell.

This building was already set out as a repair garage and a small office block was immediately added to the Wakefield Road end of the building.

Ernest Crump's only son, Bob joined the company after completing his national service in 1952. At the age of 22 he was set on as the company's first salesman with a view to increasing the number of Fodens on the roads of West Yorkshire. His task was made easier by the large motorway building projects of the fifties and sixties. Early sales success in these areas earned Foden its reputation as foremost supplier of vehicles to the construction industry.

Ernest Crump died in 1968 leaving the business to his son Bob. By 1980 the Bell Hill site had trebled in size and employed more than 50 people. The Gardner engine reconditioning business was in decline and the company had moved into the manufacture of specialist marine generating sets for trawlers and small ships. Initially this business was based on the Gardner engine but this later changed to incorporate Cummins and Caterpillar engines.

In 1980 Pelican's main supplier Foden went into receivership and was subsequently bought by the American multinational Paccar. Paccar owned Kenworth and Peterbuilt in America and wanted to expand in to the European market. After the initial uncertainty surrounding the take over confidence was restored as Paccar made the

Above: A copy of Foden News from 1940, with a feature about Pelican Engineering. Facing page top: An advertisement from February 1936 featuring a Foden rigid vehicle of the day. Facing page bottom: Pelican Engineering premises on Pepper Road, Hunslet.

The Foden S20 of the 1950's was a class leader in it's day despite the fact that the cab was bolted directly to the chassis, the driver sat right beside the Gardner LW engine with virtually no noise insulation and it was not thought necessary to supply the truck with windscreen wipers! Today's trucks are radically different; the latest "Alpha" range of trucks from Foden have levels of refinement comparable to that of a family car and are produced to meet operators exact requirements; anything less would be unsaleable.

necessary investments to guarantee the future of Foden. The concept of specialist vehicle building was introduced to the UK market for the first time. The company was able to steadily increase its Foden business in the eighties culminating in the sale of a record 350 Fodens in 1989.

In 1996 Bob Crump decided to settle for an easier life and handed over control to his son Richard who presently manages the company. Pelican now has subsidiary companies at Knottingley, Sheffield and Barnetby. Turnover has risen to £20 million and over 100 people are now employed.

The company has had to respond to changing customer requirements. When Ernest Crump founded the firm the word "credit" was largely unheard of where as now virtually all business is done on account. As the truck buying market has swung away from outright purchasing of vehicles, Pelican has had to develop its leasing, contract hire and finance business. Gone are the days when customers would tolerate their supplier closing at 5.30pm, the workshop is open 24 hours a day and has expanded into all makes repair service, body work and chassis straightening.

The trucks too have changed dramatically.

The reputation of Pelican is inextricably linked to that of Foden in Yorkshire. Pelican is the longest standing Foden dealer and looks forward to selling the marque far into the future.

Despite the increased size of the company, it is still a family firm where all the staff are appreciated as part of a team. Many of them have worked at Pelican for more than 20 years. Now in the hands of third generation management, the company plans to move to bigger and better premises and expand with Foden into the next century.

Above: A front view of the Bell Hill premises in 1979.
Below: One of the new Alpha rigid tippers.

Leeds & Bradford Boiler Company - a turnkey package

According to a handwritten journal by Herbert Hattersley Pickard, eldest son of David and Eliza Ellen Pickard, the Leeds and Bradford Boiler Company was founded in 1876 by David Midgley (sic). Mr Midgley made boilers, principally vertical boilers for local crane makers. He also made brewing pans for public houses in the days when each of them brewed their own beer.

After a time, Mr Midgley took an order for two large Galloway boilers destined for Egypt. He had insufficient capital to carry out this order. However, he had bought the sheet plates for it from Depleges in which firm R S Dower was a partner.

When he found he could not complete the order, Mr Midgley made an assignment to Depleges at twelve shillings in the pound. So, the contract was completed and the business was continued.

After being in business 16 years Mr Midgley ran into financial difficulties. He had employed a Mr Barker Oxley from Spurr Inman and Company in Wakefield who was too inexperienced for his post. Under his direction, the firm made a loss because he charged too little for the finished work. After three years of losses he was given notice.

Another factor in the firm's failure to make money was that foreman Tom Waterton's wage was made dependent on the number of men working under him. He succumbed to the temptation of taking on more than the firm could find employment for.

At this time, welding, riveting and caulking was all done by hand in an overcrowded, poorly lit workshop.

In 1892 the Pickard family became involved. David Pickard, together with Bob Dower, and both great great grandfathers of the company's present managing director, stepped in to help and the family has been the majority

Top left: *David Pickard, director from 1892 to 1918.*
Top right: *A settling tank being delivered to ICI.*
Left: *City Square, 1922.*

the factory was called Woodnook Boiler Works, it being in the Woodnook area of Stanningley. There, with steel as their raw material, the workers used hydraulic presses, plate rolls, furnaces and riveting machines.

The company made vulcanisers for the rubber industry and over the years developed the designs of their autoclaves for other applications.

A major factor in the prosperity of the company was the contribution made by H Maurice H Pickard, a notable inventor who, during his working life took out over 100 patents. He invented the "Quicklock" (registered trade mark) door for autoclaves, together with a whole collection of safety interlock devices and systems, three of which are mandatory on all autoclaves manuactured today.

A catalogue from the forties shows a range of fascinating products using these inventions, that throw light on the nature of heavy industry of the time.

In 1956 the company received a telephone call from Yorkshire Indigo. They had, they said, a Lancashire

shareholder ever since. Owing money to Depleges, Dower and Pickard bought the company and Mr Midgley ceased his interest. The list of people who had originally invested was long and included such well known names as Henry Berry and Job Isles. David Pickard's son Herbert, whose journal is so interesting and gives fascinating details of the company's transactions in his day, married Bob Dower's daughter. He was put in to run the boiler company. (Previously he had been employed in dyeing textiles, though, unfortunately, he was colour blind! As the company survived and prospered, he was obviously better suited to boiler making.) Herbert was in daily contact with friends and acquaintances in engineering for advice until he had learned the job. Later, he was to name his son Henry after Henry Berry who had given him so much help in the early days. A Mr Miles, a Sheffield man taken on as manager, had experience not only in boiler making but in the construction of pressure vessels. Through his contact the company obtained an order for a large number of vessels for the soap trade.

In the beginning the company made boilers, process plant and chemical and tar stills at the site in Stanningley where the work still goes on. The premises are in Beechwood Street and

Above: Herbert Hattersley Pickard (centre) on an employees outing in the early 1930s. Below: A steam accumulator manufactured in 1917.

Boiler, number 1080, made in 1896 for Fawcetts of Leeds. They wanted to know exactly what it was made of because it was in such good condition and was still doing quite adequately the job for which it had been designed. The company found the original specification for this boiler. the plates were made of Clydesdale Mild Steel. They were pleased to supply this information and accept the credit for such a good record for both the firm's raw materials and its sound workmanship.

HM Chief Inspector of Factories considered the company's designs so outstanding from the safety aspect that he asked to have, on permanent loan, a small autoclave incorporating the Quicklock door, protected by the company's safety devices. It was followed by a similar request from the Indian Factory Department for their new Safety Institute in Bombay.

As a result of these developments the Leeds and Bradford Boiler Company became world leaders in their field and in 1967 received the Queen's Award for Exports.

On one occasion, the company supplied 56 autoclaves to Heinz. One wonders what container was used for the 57th variety!

The company has been run by five generations of the

Pickard family which has given it long term stability. Throughout 120 years the company has adapted its skills to match the advance of the engineering technology of the day and still continues to invest in the latest machinery. This includes hot and cold pressing and spinning equipment and the firm supplies a comprehensive range of dished and flanged ends to pressure vessel manufacturers. They also have a number of horizontal and vertical borers, including three 12' 0" diameter machines fitted with profile turning attachments. They offer a subcontract machining service to the engineering industry.

Attention to product design and the use of computers ensure that the company continues to be a leader in the autoclave industry. Their Boilerclave® is used in the majority of Investment Casting foundries throughout the world. The Thermoclave® has been developed for curing composite materials for the Aerospace and motor racing industries and incorporates sophisticated computerised controls and recording equipment.

The workforce recognises that quality is created and maintained by people. The company holds the significant approval of the American A.S.M.E. 'U' stamp and the German TUV standard. The real commitment to quality is accepted as a personal and collective responsibility throughout the company.

Top: The steam accumulators on route to Lancashire.
Above right: *Maurice Pickard.* **Left:** *Thermoclave supplied to Pilkington Aerospace.*

John Catlow & Son Haulage Contractors (Est 1870)
From generation to generation

In 1870, John Catlow came to Leeds from Burnley, Lancashire in order to set up in business as a Coal Merchant and Cartage Contractor at Westfield Road. An astute man, he managed to progress fairly rapidly.

Horses were then of course the only means of transport and he very quickly possessed half a dozen or more. He then built his own premises, stable and yard for about twenty horses and carts with adjacent houses, including two cottages for his foreman and housekeeper.

Coal was the mainstay of his business and he was successful in obtaining contracts to supply most of the well established manufacturers along the north bank of the river and several south of the river with industrial fuel.

John Catlow dabbled in local politics and fought the old West Ward, Leeds as a Conservative, albeit unsuccessfully.

He was a religious man who gave a considerable amount of time to the Methodist Church.

To this day there are still a number of foundation stones bearing the name John Catlow.

Charles Alfred Catlow

Following John's death, his son Charles Alfred inherited the business and in a very short space of time increased the number of horses to fifty. However, with the outbreak of war in 1914, the War Office commandeered half the livestock for war duties, which was a severe blow to the business. Charles managed to recover by commandeering his own sense of humour, Yorkshire grit and determination. The offices were moved to nearby Wellington Street.

Alfred Catlow

In 1914, Charles' son, Alfred joined the army. After four years active service in the Middle East he was demobbed and joined the family business. Full of enthusiasm and new ideas Alfred believed the time had come to mechanise the transportation. At first his ideas

were met with some resistance from his father. At about this time the company moved again, across the road to the coal yard, which is now the site of the Yorkshire Post building. However the first petrol lorry (an AEC) was purchased in 1919. Charles Alfred died in 1944 leaving Alfred to continue with the firm.

John Douglas Catlow

Alfred's only son John, joined the company in 1947 after completing his National Service. The firm became limited in 1954 and John took over as Managing Director.

As industry changed, the demand for coal lessened. Under John's guiding hand the company diversified into the field of

general haulage and the business continued to grow, forming contracts with the building, timber and scaffolding trade.

In 1964 the company moved to the present premises at Scotch Park Trading Estate, Armley when the Yorkshire Post buildings were being planned.

The company fortunately managed to 'weather' the recession of the 1970s and 1980s by again applying Yorkshire grit and determination to succeed.

Richard Charles Catlow

John's younger son, Richard joined the family firm after leaving school in 1978. After serving his apprenticeship in HGV motor mechanics at MOTEC, Scotland, Richard worked alongside the garage foreman. At the age of 21 he passed the HGV Class I test and went out on the road as a driver.

Since 1990, Richard has worked in the office and following his father's retirement in 1995, became the fifth generation of Catlows to take control of the business.

Although the company bears little resemblance to the one started by John Catlow in 1870, it still remains a family business. It is probably this keen family interest, combined with excellent staff, and customer relations, that has helped the company grow and become a respected business in Leeds for five generations.

Above: A 1940s wagon.
Left: A coal wagon being loaded in the 1950s.
Facing page, top left: John Catlow, founder of the company.
Facing page, bottom: The first motorised wagon bought by Alfred Catlow in 1919.
Below: Richard Catlow (right) with one of today's fleet. Bert Shaw (left), foreman for thirty years and now retired.

CMA - *Motor auction pioneers*

Records are few and memories hazy, but the first purpose-built car auction in Europe, Central Motor Auctions, Rothwell appears to have begun when two business men from Doncaster, Messers and Fullers, opened a general auction site in South Accommodation Road, Leeds in 1920. What is known of the company at this time is that they were general auctioneers, holding two auctions a week - one day horses, cycles, bric-a-brac and motor spares - the other day motor vehicles.

At about the same time, local businessman, Jesse Lightfoot, started an auction in Holm Street, adjacent to Messers and Fullers, which came to be called Central Motor Auction Mart, and the two traded side by side for many years. In 1945 Lightfoot acquired the business and premises from Messers and Fullers and about a year later the joint business was purchased by two business partners, Eric Myers and Charles Franks. Previously Eric Myers and his father Joe were involved in a

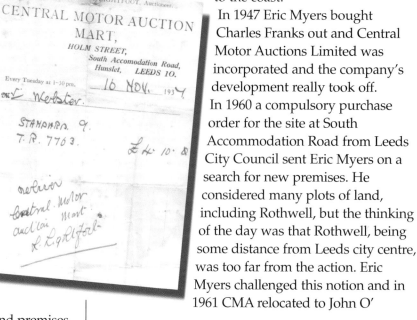

number of businesses including one, *Myers Wrose Tours of Baildon*, a coach operator still fondly remembered in North Bradford for their popular 'chara' trips to the coast.

In 1947 Eric Myers bought Charles Franks out and Central Motor Auctions Limited was incorporated and the company's development really took off.

In 1960 a compulsory purchase order for the site at South Accommodation Road from Leeds City Council sent Eric Myers on a search for new premises. He considered many plots of land, including Rothwell, but the thinking of the day was that Rothwell, being some distance from Leeds city centre, was too far from the action. Eric Myers challenged this notion and in 1961 CMA relocated to John O'

Above: Invoice dated 1937 for a Standard 9 with registration number TR 7763.
Below: The site at South Accommodation Road only days before the move to John O' Gaunts in 1961.

Gaunts, opposite the pub of the same name. The site of 13 acres came with planning permission which offered plenty of potential for expansion.

Eric Myers' instinct, that city centre siting for the motor auction trade was not essential, was backed up by his investment in the business and led to the building of the first purpose-built motor auction in Europe. With business flourishing at the home base in Leeds, Eric and his son, Anthony, set their sites further afield and opened a site in Yarm, Middlesbrough. In 1966 they expanded into Leicestershire and four years later, in 1970, they purchased T E Pilkington & Sons in Manchester. During this time Eric and Anthony identified a service they could offer to their trade clients. They pioneered multi-deck transporters for motor auctioneers, collecting and delivering multiple units bought at auction to motor traders. Another first for CMA! Long serving members of staff recall that these early transporters were left unmarked so that local traders could keep their suppliers a closely guarded secret.

In the early seventies, the Myers' identified another opportunity and set up CAM Transport, a subsidiary based at Bruntcliffe Lane, Morley. Operating nationally, a fleet of 80 vehicle transporters serviced the new and used car industry so successfully that a new headquarters opened in Britannia Road, Morley.

> "RECORDS SHOW THAT IN 1975 A FIVE YEAR OLD MINI CLUBMAN WAS SELLING FOR £400 AND A TWO YEAR OLD MERCEDES FOR £2,400"

*Top left: 'Leaving do' for long serving employee, Bernard Proctor after more than 50 years with the company. **Above:** A classic sports convertible under scrutiny before going under the hammer. **Left:** An early Seddon Transporter outside Yarm Auction in the early 1960s.*

At its height, CAM not only served its own CMA auction group, but also boasted such names as Nissan, BMW and Rover on their list of customers for new vehicle distribution.

Once again, having set the standard, CAM were followed by the competition. As enterprising as ever, Eric looked for ways to adapt and innovate once again. They spotted the potential to auction plant and machinery to be sold at auction, and the Bruntcliffe Lane site was given over to the new trade.

Through this time Eric Myers was partnered by his son Anthony who, having trained at his fathers side, became Group Managing Director. Sadly at the very early age of 41 years, Anthony died, and Eric Myers was left to take up the reins once more. A further period of expansion followed, with operations opening in Worksop, Bracknell and later Glasgow, and another local site being developed in Bradford.

In 1986 another milestone was reached when CMA went public on the unlisted securities market. Later, the first multi-storey auction centre was opened in Wimbledon. On the local front, the firm's head office, Bradford Auction, Morley Plant and Machinery Auction and Rothwell Auction were consolidated at the Rothwell site in 1991, following the purchase of an additional 13 acres of land. The next five years saw further expansion which included the acquisition of a vehicle storage site at St. Albans.

In 1993 the family and the company suffered another personal loss when Eric Myers died suddenly following a stroke. In 1996, now fully listed on the UK stock exchange, the company was bought in a joint venture deal between the Bailey family of Bristol and Manheim Auctions of America. In 1998, the holding company, Independent Car Auctions (Holdings) Ltd acquired BRS Auctions and the National Car Auction Group, thus making CMA part of a nationwide 17-centre group. The name of Myers continues at CMA with Nigel Myers, son of Anthony who remains a director of the enlarged group.

Above: A row of transporters and centre, a 'Tea-pot' Scammell Pioneer Recovery Vehicle.
Left: Anthony Myers presents his father, Eric with a silver bridge set at The Fleet Motor Show on CMA celebrating its Silver Jubilee in 1981.

John Stansfeld - the company certain to survive the millennium

In Jackson's Guide to Leeds, published in 1889, John Stansfeld is already referred to as 'One of the oldest established and largest ironmongers in Yorkshire'. His warehouse, in Alfred Street, Boar Lane, contained upward of 2,000 tons of bar iron, plates, sheets, hoop-iron and so on.

All kinds of nuts, bolts, chains, nails and other sundries were available, together with carriage, cart, van and elliptic springs, axles and bent timber.

He was well known locally for his excellent service to his customers and strangers soon knew his name because 'the most conspicuous object as one enters Leeds by the North Eastern or Midland is his monster sign in New Station Street, which covers up the whole of one side of his immense girder warehouse.

Change of ownership
Mr Stansfeld had set up his business in 1857 selling goods he manufactured from steel and wood and based at premises grandly entitled Stansfeld Chambers. He was joined in his business by his elder son, another John and a younger one.

One of the then employees, the office junior was a Jack Horner, in his first job on leaving school. Records show that he started on 1st January 1930. He well remembers the high stool and large pedestal desk with the large hand ledgers in copperplate writing. The war came and he left temporarily to do service overseas. At the end of the war he returned to Stansfelds and eventually bought the business from the Stansfeld family with David Bolton.

Today David, now retired, has a son called Tony, who is a director of the company. Managing Director is Malcolm Rogerson, Mr Horner's son-in-law. Mr Horner is now 82 and still takes an active interest in the company, passing his expert eye over every invoice going out to customers.

Some years ago when challenged on a weight on a wagon, the company pleaded in mitigation that it had not offended before, according to records, and the only case from memory was with one of its horse-drawn loads when a large steel joist became wedged through the company's archway, the rest of the bar blocking all of Great George Street!

The company now with a new modern catalogue and fully computerised is well prepared for the millennium, is quality assured and has a wide customer base, covering most industrial estates in radius, covering many industries including food, building and construction, furniture, printing, chemical, motor, sheet metal and the gate and railings industry.

Above: A cover of a brochure issued at the turn of the century.
Left: An early picture of the premises.

Almost a century young and still growing

After serving throughout the first world war, Mr William Henry Young came home from the Army to his wife Harriet Maud. Together they set up their own business.

Surprisingly for those days, Mrs Young was a stalwart of the firm, travelling round the industrial West Riding as a company representative.

As a commercial traveller she was in a tough position. Both her rivals and the firms with whom she wished to trade probably thought her place should have been at home cooking her husband's supper. However, she was not deterred but went about her business.

Growth through determination

Since the business at that time did not run to a company car, she travelled by train, bus or on foot, visiting shops in Castleford, Pontefract, Normanton, Featherstone and Wakefield. The samples of sweets she had to show them were carried in two large bags, one under each arm. She could hardly have been comfortable as she trudged miles in good weather and bad.

Through her efforts trade increased. From its small beginnings in a tiny building in King's Street, Leeds centre, its only transport a horse and cart, the firm became a limited company, operating a warehouse in Gibson Street, Burmanstofts, Leeds. From these premises the company moved to Pontefract Lane in 1961, the year following Robert Furness' death. The building they used there had been the Friends' Adult School. Mr Robert Furness, one of its students, was the Youngs' nephew. He came to work for his uncle and aunt, becoming managing director after the Second World War and taking over the business when William and Harriet retired.

A family business

More of the family followed him into the business. After his death his widow became managing director, his son Jack became a director and secretary and his son in law, Kenneth Marchant became the sales director in charge of the sales force, toys and non-foods. Daughter Barbara Marchant worked in the toy department, whilst daughter in law Sheila Furness worked in the office and dealt with the wages.

In 1974 the Youngs moved to the Cross Green Trading Estate and achieved a turnover that year of £750,000 and the firm began to be reckoned with in the world of cash and carry and wholesale distribution. Barbara Furness was very proud of their fully-computerised firm.

Expansion

Twelve years later, in the mid eighties the firm opened a new 4,000 square feet extension to house all its non-food products such as toys and stationery. It made procedures much easier, allowing food and non-food sections to run on two different floors.

The eighties were a time when many large firms were being swallowed up by even larger conglomerates in rushed stock-exchange take-over deals

Above: One of the company's vans, dating from the 1960s.
Facing page, top: William Henry Young, founder.
Facing page, bottom: Ken and Barbara Marchant in the 1950s.
Below: Lynn Marchant (now Bell) with a giant easter egg in 1962. Lynn is now a Director.

but Jack Furness and Ken Marchant were determined to keep their firm in the hands of their families. Nevertheless it was sensible to band together with other independents and for this purpose, Key Distribution was formed. It had a centralised computer in Nottingham which allowed participating companies to standardise their invoices to large concerns.

Remaining a family concern enabled Youngs to make their own economies when they felt them necessary, to make decisions on the spot without having to refer to a head office and, most important, to maintain personal contact with their customers.

Although Youngs sold to large multi-nationals such as off-license chain Peter Dominic, it also

supplied local off licenses, confectioners and traders. At this time, they operated both a cash and carry system and an order and delivery service, backed up by six sales representatives and a telesales team who made contact with shops to ensure that their orders were delivered in time.

Traders were moving away from direct trading and were beginning to use Youngs as their supplier, taking smaller stocks and using the extra cash which had been frozen as stock to improve their cash flow. Mr Jack Furness, director in the eighties was happy to go along with this new development.

And today...

W H & H M Young Limited are currently one of the eleven firms under the umbrella of Key Lekkerland Ltd of Rugby, Warwickshire. There the parent company has a computer system common to all the depots and linked to mainland Europe. Coping well with the competition from many local firms, the stock offered to customers includes confectionery, crisps and snacks, soft drinks, alcohol, groceries and chilled and frozen foods. Tobacco was introduced to the range in 1972, as were toys, though the supplying of toys ceased in 1997.

A large part of the West Riding and the East Coast was covered when Youngs were quite

a small concern. the increasing extent of the motorway networks means that now they can deliver to most of the north of England. Proud of the beginning of their delivery service by horse and cart, Youngs are even prouder of their present fleet of lorries which includes two seven-ton, three twelve-ton and seven seventeen-ton vehicles. Three vehicles are needed to cope with Youngs' Slush Puppie franchise for Yorkshire and Humberside.

Already Youngs are the main suppliers to many convenience stores, off-licenses, schools, colleges and universities, forecourts and leisure outlets. Their aim is total supply through the EDI link. New premises will be taken as this becomes necessary, hopefully together with electronic warehousing. The site for it, opposite the present one, at 3.75 acres has already been bought. Mrs Babs Furness, who took over as managing director when her husband Bob died in 1960, has now retired to live in Spain. Now aged 86 she fondly remembers the Christmas clubs that Youngs ran in the thirties, the fire that brought disaster to the firm in 1937 when her husband was injured in his attempt to stop the blaze taking hold, and the time during the second war when the warehouse contained only a 4lb box of Bellamys'

sweets. In the new millennium Youngs look forward to their own centenary and hers under the fourth generation of family directors - Lee Furness (Managing Director) and Lynn Bell (Director).

Above: Managing director, Barbara Furness presents customer, Rod Brown with a stereo system at the opening of the cash-and-carry at Cross Green. *Facing page, top:* Jack Furness presents an easter egg at a candy ball at the Capital Ballroom in Leeds, in the 1950s. *Facing page, bottom:* Barbara Furness helps with picking orders. *Below:* Members of Key Lekkerland presentation by Mars for turnover achievement in 1992.

Granary Wharf - adapting the past for the needs of the future

Leeds Canal Basin lies at the junction of the Aire and Calder Navigation and the Leeds and Liverpool Canal. For many years it was a forgotten area, lying neglected and derelict beneath Leeds City Station. However, recent developments on the site have started to bring it back into public awareness.

When the Leeds section of the Leeds and Liverpool Canal was opened in 1777, the Leeds Mercury reported that, 'the concourse of people was innumerable, the greatest perhaps that was ever assembled on any such occasion in the kingdom.

Now, more than two hundred years later, the crowds are starting to return, to wander through the new craft market and rediscover a site that played an important part in the development of Leeds and which has always been on their doorstep.

The 127 miles long Leeds and Liverpool Canal is the longest single canal in Britain. It was built between 1770 and 1816. In conjunction with the Aire and Calder Navigation it was a major factor in the growth of industrial Leeds in the 19th century. Together they provided a trans-Pennine link between two major trading ports, Liverpool and Hull, from where goods were imported and exported all over the world.

Raw materials for the construction of the factories and mills in the Holbeck area were unloaded at the Canal Basin. Then, following the completion of the mills and the factories which were mainly for the textile industry, the Canal Basin was the unloading point for raw flax and wool.

In addition, the Canal Basin, being considerably larger than it is today, was used as a centre for the construction, repair and maintenance of canal boats.

However, during the late 19th century it came under increasing pressure from an innovation in transport,

At home, the canal provided a cheap and easy method of transport between the West Riding and the manufacturing towns of Lancashire.

The Canal Basin developed quickly as a distribution and storage centre for a variety of goods, Coal, cotton and slate were a few of the commodities besides flax and wool were processed here, which helped the canal become one of the most prosperous in the country.

Above: The Granary building and canal basin circa 1970.
Right: Dark Arches entrance in the **1960s.**

There was virtually no traffic after 1930 and the Leeds Waterfront became derelict and redundant.

So it remained until the early seventies. It was then acquired by Leda Securities who recognised the future potential of the site for refurbishment and development.

Initially the Canal Basin and the Dark Arches were used mainly for small workshops and for storage, particularly for the motor trade. Before this the Arches had been used for many years as storage for local companies. One of them, Joseph Watson & Sons, (known as Soapy Joe's), occupied a series of arches at the west end of the complex. The bulk of the stored materials were highly flammable, resin, tallow and oil. In January 1892 a fire broke out in the Arches. It was extinguished the following day at the cost of one life, that of a fireman who fell into the flames as 1500 tons of goods were consumed. The iron bridge across the Monk Pit area of the canal was destroyed, along with the railway line

the railways. Both were in competition for the same trade and inevitably the railways, which were faster and cheaper won out. In the Leeds Canal Basin the rail network encroached on more and more of the site and today the trains still clatter over the arches, past the now quiet waters.

By the turn of the century the railways had completely overtaken the canals as the major means of internal transportation. and the decline of the Canal Basin can be dated from that time.

During the seventies the area was upgraded for use as small industrial units. This was extended to the south side of the canal when the Vicars area was acquired in the eighties.

In 1987 Leda Securities entered into a joint venture with British Waterways to take the development of the site forward. The first step was to obtain planning permission, making it possible to extend the existing industrial uses to accommodate craft workshops and small business developments. The focus was being moved from industry to the retail sale of artefacts made by local craftsmen.

It seemed in the long term that the waterfront had the potential for tourism development on the back of specialist retail and leisure outlets. In 1987 a plan was submitted to the council to establish the Festival Market Place under the Dark Arches for retail use together with a weekend craft market. Written in was the facility to run events on the waterfront and provide street entertainment which presently includes music, dance, juggling, theatre and regular children's entertainment.

At that time the Canal Basin was only being used as a tourist venue at weekends since the public saw the Dark Arches as being too far away from the city centre. The Canal Basin Agency, however, felt that, if it could sustain Granary Wharf as a retail and leisure venue, then eventually the city would develop south of the

railway viaduct, bringing with it a new clientele needing full time leisure and retail facilities. Granary Wharf has therefore been developed in its own right as well as being part of the Leeds Development Corporation's and now Leeds City Council's plan to regenerate and expand the city centre.

Today a number of schemes are being put into effect at the Basin, with the aim of providing an attractive area for both visitors and the people of Leeds. The new scheme is a millennium face-lift for the area, maintaining and rehousing existing tenants into refurbished space and providing new facilities for the office workers during lunchtime and early evening. The aim is to have everything complete by 2000. In the meantime the shops, stalls and entertainment will continue, albeit with some temporary disruption.

The site is rich in canal history and to encompass this an environmental trail is being developed which will be accessible to all members of the community. Work at the Canal Basin is not aimed at fossilising the area but at adapting the past for the needs of the future.

The Granary Wharf management feels that the Holbeck area has been overlooked by the LDC, but it is now being recognised as the centre for a potential urban village.

Both pictures: Since the formation of the Granary Wharf Festival, Market Place entertainment and events have taken place every weekend and will continue to do so during the period of refurbishment.

Corn Exchange - speciality shopping under one roof

In 1860 the local council of Leeds decided to commission a new building that would house both the sale of corn in sacks and the sale of corn by sample. The old Corn Exchange at the top of Briggate was too small, dark and generally outdated. The commission to build the new one was given to Cuthbert Brodrick from Hull because his work on the Leeds Town Hall had been so satis-

factory. The council explained their requirements, that the building should fit the available site and let in the maximum amount of light so that the goods on offer could be properly examined.

The building officially opened for trade in 1863. It is one of the finest specimens of Leeds architecture. The exterior is faced with diamond pointed

The Corn Exchange - 191

stonework, broken by regularly repeated arches housing two storeys of windows. There is a beautifully modelled garlanded frieze and the two porticoes swell out of the building in contrasting curves.

Inside, the painted brickwork repeats the pattern of the arches on three floors. Each arch represented a corn merchant's office. Over the whole space the glass domed roof rises 75 feet above floor level at its highest point. The elliptical shape of the plan of the Exchange was influenced by the need to fit it into

> ## "THE BUILDING OFFICIALLY OPENED IN 1863, ONE OF THE FINEST SPECIMENS IN LEEDS"

the irregularly shaped site beside the White Cloth Hall and the former Assembly rooms.

As the use of the Corn Exchange market declined over the years, the building fell into disrepair. In 1988 Speciality Shops plc won a nationwide competition to redevelop the Corn Exchange as a speciality shopping centre. The company spent more than four million pounds in refurbishment and has replaced the unstable ground floor and restored the glazed dome roof to its original state. It is a Grade 1 Listed building and all plans for changes to it must be strictly overseen by the authorities responsible.

The corn traders who today number 25 continued to trade throughout the refurbishment and still meet in the building every Tuesday. They are not as active as 125 years ago but are still very important. On the main floor of the Corn Exchange, the by-laws that continue to regulate the corn traders' market are still displayed. The original Victorian lectern and corn traders' tables are still in use.

In the dome of the Corn Exchange the Kitty Hawk Flyer (Wright Flyer 1) is displayed. This is a model of the aircraft built by Wilbur and Orville Wright on which they achieved the first successful powered and controlled human flight in a heavier than air craft at Kitty Hawk, North Carolina. The Wright brothers conceived, designed, built and flew the first plane. It is believed that this model, constructed in 1966 was built by airmen of RAF Finningley as an 8.000 man-hour project. This reproduction was flown 20 feet in trials in an effort to replicate Wilbur Wright's original flight of 852 feet in 59 seconds.

Speciality Shops worked closely with the Leeds City Council to create an exciting shopping environment and to enable a tradition of trading to be reborn. This practice will be continued by the new owners - Arcadia Limited.

Left: The building as it was in 1913.

Big oaks from little acorns grow

James Greenwood worked in a hatter's shop in Westgate, Bradford. The shop's owner was deeply in debt, disappeared in 1860 and was never seen again. James Greenwood acquired the shop and, with the help of his 12 year old son Moses continued the business.

In 1865 the premises were demolished for road widening. James retired but Moses found another shop in Westgate and continued trading from there, opening in October of the same year. The first day's takings were nine shillings and twopence. In the flickering light of gas jets Moses made and renovated hats for the wool barons of Bradford.

In another shop, still in Westgate, business improved and Moses began to sell straw hats as well as the silk ones that were the mainstay of the trade. When his son Willie joined the firm he persuaded his father to stock other items of menswear. He cycled to Holts, the Leeds wholesaler, where he bought ties and braces. Later on he also introduced shirts and stiff white collars.

The family lived above the shop and it was there that Mr Walter Greenwood and his two brothers were born. In 1903 Willie took over the shop next door and had a new shop front installed. He opened every day except Sunday, Good Friday and Christmas Day. The hours worked were nine in the morning till eight at night from Monday to Thursday. On Friday closing was at 10 pm and on Saturdays he closed at midnight.

Walter Greenwood came into the business in 1919. Two years later another premises was taken giving the shop a corner site with a frontage of 80 feet. Walter was anxious for the business to grow. Several branches were opened including one in London that was not successful. In 1927 Walter took over the branches leaving his father and brother with the main shop and warehouse. Soon he had shops in Sunderland, Middlesborough, Skipton and Heckmondwyke. Head Office and warehouse was one room above a branch in Manchester Road, Bradford, and transport was one Morris Oxford car. He did all his own window dressing, stocktaking and buying and by 1932 had 26 shops. When his father retired, Walter took the Westgate shop back as his headquarters. One brother started a hat factory in Preston and the other worked for Walter.

During the war no new branches were opened, two were bombed out and several badly damaged. Following the war expansion continued and during the forties Walter's sons Denis and Brian joined him.

In 1952 the 100th branch was opened and four years later the foundation stone was laid for the present Head Office and warehouse at White Cross, Guiseley. By the time Walter died in 1971 the company had 261 shops with the two brothers being joint managing directors and co-chairmen.

> **"IN 1952 THE 100TH BRANCH OF GREENWOODS WAS OPENED"**

In the eighties it was decided to split the business into two parts. Denis kept the Greenwood chain of shops and Brian took the other assets of the group. Many changes were made in the style of shop fitting and the furnishings in the branches and head office. During a period of recession some smaller branches were closed. Others were lost due to the advent of out of town shopping and changes of street patterns.

In 1996 a new management team headed by John Hanson took over the running of the company and many changes have taken place since then. A programme of shop closures was accelerated to clear out all unwanted branches whilst new ones were opened in Liverpool, Carlisle, Rochdale and Scarborough.

The policy of aiming for the middle market in terms of age, fashion and price has been continued along with the concept of giving the best possible value, backed by service to the customer.

Facing page, top: The original shop in Bradford.
Facing page, bottom: Moses Greenwood, at work in the 1870s.
Below: One of the firm's shops today.

Ross Fabrics - sixty five years old and still going strong

Sims Ross (pictured left), father of the present Chairman of Ross Fabrics was born in 1900 and set up S Ross & Co Limited in 1933. His premises in Leeds were at the corner of Wade Lane and Rockingham Street on which now stands the Thistle Hotel, part of the Merrion Centre.

His business was trading in upholstery sundries, which he had learned about from his earlier employers.

At that time he had a bookkeeper Mrs Joan Myers and a counter assistant Jimmy Hemingway, who was later called up to serve in the RAF, but returned to the Company immediately after the War. Mr Ross's son Michael, the present Chairman, joined the family firm after leaving Leeds Grammar School in 1955. In those days the Company premises were situated in St Paul's Street, Leeds, the exact location being at the top of Queen Street on which now stands the Carlton Tower building.

By this time the Company employed five people. It now traded in upholstery fabrics as well as sundries and Jimmy Hemingway was the proud driver of a Morris Minor Traveller, seeking business further afield in places such as Hull, Sheffield and Nottingham.

In the late 1960s the firm moved to a former Methodist Chapel on Churwell Hill, Morley and later to their present 30,000 square feet premises in Leeds.

Sims Ross in his first office in Wade Lane

Michael Ross still retains a pair of cutting scissors and a yard stick from his father's original premises in Wade lane.

It was during the years in Churwell that the Company expanded and Michael, having started at the bottom sweeping the warehouse floors, looking after the coke boiler and cutting and rolling cloth, began to put his experiences to good use. His father became ill in the late 1960s, when he took on all the responsibilities of running a Company and being an employer. His ultimate plan was to take a small Company started by his father in 1933 Public, which he did in 1981.

Unfortunately his father died in 1972, never seeing how far his son had taken the Company. During his years of founding and running the Company, Sims Ross had a high reputation for honesty and integrity and Michael believes his father could not have left him anything better than that reputation.

Since going Public in 1981 the Company has continued to prosper and is now a major player in the UK, distributing fabrics throughout the country. It offers its customers a combination of excellent product, value for money, reliable service and a vast wealth of knowledge and experience.

Although taken over in 1995, the Company continues to grow in the modern business world whilst at the same time retaining traditional values.

One of many things Michael Ross learned during his early days with the firm was the importance of treating all people with respect whether it be suppliers, employees or customers.

Above: An early business card.
Below: Members of Ross Fabric's Sales Team at a recent Exhibition. Seated front left Max Brasher (Sales Director), centre Michael Ross (Chairman), right Laurence Silver (Managing Director).

PHONE LEEDS 25109

GRAMS 25109 LEEDS 1

S. Ross & Co Ltd.
2, West Street,
Leeds 1.
TEXTILES & TRIMMINGS

FURNISHING FABRICS
UPHOLSTERY GOODS
SUNDRIES

HESSIANS & JUTE GOODS
LEATHER-CLOTHS
PLASTIC-CLOTHS

Rothera + Brereton - over 40 years of traditional service to the printing industry

In 1949 Donald Brereton was a young lad leaving grammar school in Liverpool, applying to the Labour Exchange for a job. He wanted to be a journalist but the lady, hearing the word 'paper' sent him to L S Dixon, a local paper merchant.

He did well until he was sent off to serve his country in the second war. Afterwards he returned and by 1959 Dixons chose him to open their first Yorkshire branch in Leeds, the Liverpool company having been represented there for many years by Mr Rothera.

Four years later the two men decided to establish their own business even though Mr Rothera was by then well into his sixties. They rented premises in Fairfield House in Dewsbury Road, beginning as stockist merchants in printings and writings and serving printers in west and south Yorkshire.

The Dewsbury Road lease expired after five years so the company obtained a larger freehold site in Armley Road where it built the first bespoke merchanting warehouse in Leeds. Providing a same-day service the new warehouse set the standard for future paper merchanting operations in the area. Further extensions followed and 1976 saw the opening of Rothera + Brereton (Sheffield) Ltd.

Mr Rothera had died in 1970 and in 1984 the successful Rothera + Brereton Group decided to join Bunzl plc, a large multi-national company, being the second UK paper merchant to do so

after Donald Murray Paper. Rothera + Brereton retained its name and independence and the company is now the flagship of the Bunzl North regional organisation.

Mr Brereton described himself as a traditionalist and spent over 40 years in the business of giving printers a traditional service.

Under Mr Jeff Lewis, the current managing director, expansion has taken place in both company size and geographical area. He believes that Rothera + Brereton's success is due to its philosophy of stocking paper and board in depth and variety, with particular emphasis on coated papers and mill branded lines. "Being part of Bunzl Fine Paper has enabled us to have all the benefits of being part of a very successful group, whilst enabling us to retain our individuality and be identified by our customers as their local merchant.

Above: The office and warehouse prior to R+B extending its buildings to cope with steady growth in the last 25 years.
Facing page, top: Joint founder, Donald Brereton, now retired.
Facing page, bottom: R+B moved into its new premises despite the problem of having the end of the street still standing in the middle of its forecourt.
Below: The Paper Warehouse before racking was introduced into it. Donald Brereton is the lone figure.

Providing quality education and training for the local and wider community

Thomas Danby College is named after the first Mayor of Leeds Captain Thomas Danby of Farnley. Tradition has it he was something of a colourful character who used his position and wealth to become the first Mayor.

Charles the Second granted Leeds a Charter on the 2nd November 1661 which allowed the town sufficient money and status to elect a Mayor to assist the 12 aldermen and 24 assistants.

Thomas Danby

Captain Danby came from a long established, powerful local family and was an officer in the Royal Army. He was selected as an alderman on the 4th January 1662, at the fourth sitting of the Town Council after reputedly using his power and money to influence the decision. This was the final vital step in an orchestrated plan to become Mayor, to which office he was elected on the 9th May 1662.

In his honour the Town Coat of Arms was changed to include three mullets. These are popularly thought to be stars but are in fact the rowels of spurs.

Danby's eye for power also extended to his marriage and he married Margaret, daughter of Colonel William Eure. This alliance helped him greatly in pursuit of the Mayoral seat, as the Eures were one of Yorkshire's longest standing and important families. His union with the Eure family helped Thomas Danby little after that for he died in a knife fight over a gambling debt at the Grays Inn, London in 1677. Margaret survived her husband by eleven years, dying without children in 1688.

There is often confusion between Captain Thomas Danby, first Mayor of Leeds and the much more famous Thomas Osborne of Danby, also referred to as Sir Thomas Osborne, the first Duke of

after taking a bribe from the East India Company.

In the reception area of Thomas Danby College is a bust, popularly believed to be of Captain Danby. In fact it is of neither he nor Sir Thomas Osborne but was a keystone in one of the buildings which had formerly occupied the same site. Apparently, builders of the new College included the bust in construction to preserve it.

It is ironic perhaps - that history has not only attributed someone else's reputation and exploits to Captain Thomas Danby but a bust in the college named after him is of someone else.

Left: Jim Watts, Chair of Governors cutting the first sod on Phase One of the construction of the College.
Facing page: St. Clement's Church was demolished to make way for the College.
Below: Dr. Brian Boffey, then Principal inside one of the diggers used in the construction of the College.

Leeds. Thomas Osborne Danby was an English Statesman and Royalist Yorkshire Landowner who lived from 1632 to 1712. Confusion between the two is probably not only because of the similarity of their names and titles but because they lived about the same time. Sir Thomas Osborne was instrumental in bringing William and Mary to the English Throne and was their first Minister. In 1694 he was made the first Duke of Leeds, continuing in parliamentary power until 1699 when he was deprived of all office

The origins of the College
The College originally emerged in the mid fifties and was then known as the Branch College of Domestic Economy. This was a time when the concept of 'Technical Colleges' was rising in popularity and many such vocational training establishments were being created all over the country.

Thomas Danby College came into being in 1970 with the formation of Polytechnics and soon after a purpose built 'Main Site' was proposed.

At the time the College was operating from five sites around the city: Czar Street (Nursery Nursing), Sweet Street (General Education), Gower Street (Catering/Baking), Whitehall Road (Meat/Catering/Hairdressing) and Portland Way (Baking/Catering).

These annexes all closed with the opening of the new building and their programmes are accommodated within the Main Site.

Construction on the present building in Roundhay Road commenced in the mid seventies and Phase One of the current site was opened in September 1977. Work on Phase Two was completed in 1980. The distinctive big orange box with its characteristic external steelwork is now

The College is recognised nationally as a Centre of Excellence for many of its programmes, which are offered full time, part time, flexible delivery and open learning. Wherever possible, it is a priority within Thomas Danby College to ensure that training can be offered to match the client's needs.

Programme areas work very closely with the industries that they serve and Thomas Danby College has excellent links with the local community. It also has many active partnerships, such as those with the local Training and Enterprise Council, and the Leeds Development Agency. The College also has associations with Higher Education institutes such as Leeds Metropolitan University, Leeds University, Huddersfield University and Ripon and York St. John. This ensures that good progression routes can be offered to all Thomas Danby College students.

widely regarded as an icon of seventies design and is frequently used in College marketing material because of it's singular style and appearance.

From its situation in Roundhay Road, the College operates in thirty one other sites throughout East Leeds and is at the centre of a multi-cultural inner-city area. The clients it serves are reflective of its location in the community.

A wide range of programmes are offered in the following areas:- Adult and Community Education, Arts and Media, Baking Technology, Business and Management, Child Care and Education, Hairdressing and Beauty Therapy, Health, Science and Food Technology, Hospitality, Humanities and Access, Information Technology, Leisure and Sport, Meat Technology, Languages, and Social Care.

"THE COLLEGE OPERATES IN 31 OTHER SITES THROUGHOUT EAST LEEDS

And today...
In recent years the College has established many new programmes, responding to clients' needs, These include Business and Management, Humanities and Access, Information Technology and Arts and Media. In fact the College's pro-active stance in the community has won it the NIACE Older and Bolder Institutional Award for good practice in estab-lished programmes, providing programmes involving older learners.

Above: A student on the College's BTEC National Certificate in Outdoor Pursuits. The only one of its kind in the country.
Facing page, top: Tim Eggar M.P. opening the College's Child Care Centre in 1991.
Facing page, bottom: The completed College (the big orange box).

Leeds Civic Theatre - a night to remember

The Leeds Civic Theatre was originally the Leeds Institute of Arts and Sciences, designed in 1868 by Cuthbert Broderick and intended as a lecture hall. However, membership of the Institute declined and the main hall was used increasingly for theatrical performances. In 1939 the Institute finally came to an end and the building was bought by the City of Leeds.

After the war the council made extensive alterations, changing the lecture hall into a proscenium theatre which became the home of amateur productions. Then in 1983 the Theatre was refurbished by Clare Ferraby who had been responsible for the magnificent restoration of the Leeds Grand Theatre. She is the Leeds-born international design consultant and head of Clare Ferraby Designs. The operation cost £70,000 and took just nine weeks to complete. The seating was increased from 444 to 530 and arranged in continental style to provide more leg room. Five thousand pounds raised by Leeds Civic Arts Guild made it possible to improve the facilities for disabled people.

Changes included rearranging the seating, reconstructing the proscenium wall and restoring the magnificent gasolier. This had been found when the old proscenium surround was removed. It was refurbished with gold leaf, crystal and lights to add a final touch of elegance.

The ceiling decoration included star stencilling, some of the stars being gilded with pure gold leaf. The colours were taken from the original tiles round the back of the side stalls and included shades of turquoise, rust, terracotta and pale blue.

A trap door and hoist were added to the stage so that scenery from the storage room below could be lifted directly on to it.

The Theatre became the home of the Leeds Civic Arts Guild, formed to affiliate the common interests of amateur cultural and artistic societies within the Leeds area. The Guild co-ordinated their activities, giving them fair shares in use of the facilities such as rehearsal rooms.

Right: *The beautiful building has become an ever more popular venue for theatre-goers.*

Consequently a wide and varied programme was presented for around 40 weeks each year. The facilities were lent to professional productions on the remaining available dates. They helped to attract new audiences whom the management hopes will become regular visitors.

The Guild's amateur productions were adjudicated by the Guild Executive Committee which

held a presentation evening every year with trophies for the best production, best actor and best set. These were presented by a civic dignatory and were keenly contested. The result was excellent entertainment in a 'proper' theatre at a fraction of the cost of other theatres in the area.

Famous people who first 'trod the boards' at the Civic include Peter O'Toole, Ron Pickup, Barry Cryer and Mark Curry.

In addition to the entertainments the Theatre was also available for conferences, seminars, meetings and functions. Being only ten minutes' walk from Leeds Intercity Railway Station and convenient for the M1 and M 62 motorways, it was a popular venue. A one-day UFO conference became so popular it was extended to become a three day event, whilst the ever-popular pantomime became a traditional family outing.

Currently 23 groups belong to the Arts Guild and perform regularly at the Theatre for 34 weeks of

the year. The remaining weeks are still taken up by professional touring companies. The main attraction is still the annual pantomime which is increasing in popularity so that in 1998-9 its run will be extended by an extra week.

Three men, a Chief Technician and two assistants are in charge of all stage set ups and scenery erection together with lighting and sound effects which all make up the end effect the audience experiences at a performance. The Civic's box office serves the City Council as the main source of ticket distribution in Leeds, selling, alongside tickets for its own productions, those for 20 international orchestras. Most other events in and around the area are also covered. The theatre is one of the few outlets for distributing the free tickets for the extremely popular Park Events hosted by Leeds City Council in the grounds of Temple Newsam and Roundhay Park.

Above: A recent production staged at Leeds Civic Theatre.
Left: The auditorium before renovations.
Below: ...and today.